Praise for *Jobs to be Don*

"What sets *Jobs to be Done* apart is that it effectively bridges the gap between customer insights and strategy. The book is filled with techniques and examples that show you not only how to bolster what you know about your customers, but also how to transform that knowledge into a concrete plan for winning in the market."

— Jon Duke, director, corporate strategy, PetSmart

"*Jobs to be Done* gives you a refreshingly straightforward means to uncover hidden customer needs, including ones that customers would struggle to tell you about on their own."

— Vijay Krish, general manager, Internet of Things, Cisco

"What I love about *Jobs to be Done* is that it goes well beyond the product. It lays out how you can use the data and knowledge you have about customers to rethink your ways of doing business and delivering value."

— Brian Newman, executive vice president, global operations, PepsiCo

"Consumers can't always tell you what will make their lives better, so you need to look deeply and thoroughly for insight. *Jobs to be Done* is a lens to understand how to innovate in a way that will capture consumer demand. All companies, regardless of size, can use the *Jobs to be Done* approach to create products that get the job done so much better for consumers that they can't wait to fire their old solutions."

— Stacy Maher Ball, director of Consumer Insights and Innovation Center of Excellence, Clorox

"In my own startups and the large customers we support, I have seen innovators re-discover the core jobs of the innovation process through painstaking trial and error—because they didn't have this book. *Jobs to be Done* is a must-have for anyone pushing the envelope or breaking the mold. Successful innovation never happens in a vacuum. *Jobs to be Done* joins the ranks of IDEO's rules of brainstorming and Agile's user stories by laying out the patterns and channels of invention. It's the kind of book you leave on your desk so you can keep coming back to it."

— John Frank, founder and CEO, Diffeo

"I love this book and I love that it's referred to as a 'roadmap.' That is exactly what this book delivers. This would be useful for any company looking for growth through innovation."

— Lisa Michaelis, chief life care officer, Mosaic Healthcare

"*Jobs to be Done* is a 'must read' for entrepreneurs. It gives you a practical, validated system to come up with new ideas or test out the ones you've already thought of."

— Nathan Eagle, founder and CEO, Jana

"*Jobs to Be Done* gives us a process that has been proven across industries, including life sciences, for re-thinking the status quo and creating transformative initiatives."

— Dr. Oliver Reuss, head of business model and healthcare innovation, Boehringer Ingelheim

"Companies too often forget to ask: "'What is the question that we're trying to answer?'" Great process around that question—of *Jobs to be Done*—enables repeatable innovation, and a consistently modern approach to developing client solutions. This book is a definitive guide to operationalize focused, creative thinking that produces outstanding results for clients, and for the companies that help them to succeed."

— Jeanette Gorgas, chief strategy officer, Grant Thornton LLP

JOBS TO BE DONE

STEPHEN WUNKER • JESSICA WATTMAN • DAVID FARBER

JOBS TO BE DONE

A ROADMAP FOR CUSTOMER-CENTERED INNOVATION

HarperCollins Leadership

An Imprint of HarperCollins

Jobs to be Done

Published by HarperCollins Leadership, an imprint of HarperCollins Focus LLC.

ISBN 978-1-4002-3876-7 (TP)

ACKNOWLEDGMENTS

Any acknowledgments for a book on Jobs to be Done must lead off with a salute to Harvard Business School Professor Clayton Christensen. Clay first popularized the idea in his 2003 book *The Innovator's Solution,* and he continues to write and speak to make this thinking well known. He mentored me at a crucial time in my career, and I was proud to work with him for six years at the consulting firm he cofounded, Innosight. My former Innosight colleague Scott Anthony also influenced my thinking, and I fondly remember our first project using Jobs to be Done to shape the specifications for a new mobile device. The road we set out on back then culminated in the Jobs Atlas that underlies this book. I also learned about the best ways to apply Jobs thinking from several clients and colleagues along the way, including Deborah Arcoleo at Hershey, Paul Conrad at Zimmer, Ken Dobler at Ethicon, Jon Duke at PetSmart, Nate Hill at Nestlé, Rajit Kamal at DePuy Synthes, Peter Lach at Barclays, Carla O'Dell at APQC, and Dan Sondee at Ingersoll Rand. We interviewed many practitioners about their experiences, and we owe many insights to Stephen Brickley, Darren Coleman, Christine Dahm, Brendan McSheffrey, Pramod Mohanlal, Hari Nair, and Trang Nguyen. Naturally, my colleagues at New Markets Advisors have been critical contributors of thoughts, examples, and critiques. Additionally, Alex Edwards provided the brilliant drawings, and both Anil Glen and Liza Swartz contributed many of the graphics. Finally, my coauthors provided so much to this book that

I couldn't possibly list the contributions. "Thank you" simply can't express the gratitude I feel.

—Stephen Wunker

Thanks and appreciation are due to many who helped make this book possible. I'm thoroughly grateful for the support and encouragement received from each and every one. My colleagues at New Markets deserve particular recognition for putting into practice many of the ideas and strategies covered in this book. Their critical insights into what works and what doesn't challenged us to refine our model and improve our ideas. The quality of this book is testament to their excellence. Further thanks go to Pramod Mohanlal, managing director of Yowzit. A true believer in the Jobs to Be Done thinking, Pramod gave us the chance to use the method to build a social enterprise in South Africa. There is no stronger litmus test of an approach than to use it yourself. Having done so, I am convinced of the utility of the Jobs to be Done lens for driving public sector innovation. Lastly, appreciation, recognition, and tremendous thanks are owed to Stephen and David. Their relentless pursuit of great ideas, enthusiasm for getting the details right, and willingness to be challenged have made writing this book a true pleasure. They are wonderful colleagues and great friends.

—Jessica Wattman

I owe an enormous amount of thanks to the many individuals who have helped shape and create this book. While there are countless people whose help and support I truly appreciate, space allows me to call out but a few by name. Several people have been quite influential in shaping the way I write. In particular, I owe a great deal of gratitude to Lawrie Bertram, whose advice I refer to daily. I also need to thank

Lynn Addington and Karen O'Connor. Their own accomplishments and publishing successes are truly inspiring. More importantly, their mentorship has been more valuable than they know. Their respective guidance in helping me craft my capstone and produce a full-length documentary has given me a set of skills that I will never stop relying on.

A number of former colleagues also deserve special mention. In particular, I want to express my sincerest thanks to Jay Jumper, John Zurawski, Kristin Lapicki, and Mel Jiganti. Beyond being some of the best in their respective fields, these individuals have been enormously influential in shaping how I approach challenges and advise clients. I also want to thank my current colleagues at New Markets. Their help has been invaluable in strengthening our arguments, finding fresh examples, and otherwise supporting us as we've balanced being both writers and consultants. In particular, I owe a great deal of thanks to my coauthors, Steve and Jessica. Their knowledge and passion have made this book what it is.

Finally, I want to thank the many friends and family members who have continuously provided help, support, and encouragement. Howie, Sheila, Greg, and Rina all deserve special thanks.

—David Farber

CONTENTS

■ CONTENTS ■

■ PART II ■

USING JOBS TO BE DONE TO BUILD GREAT IDEAS:

JOBS TO BE DONE

■ INTRODUCTION ■

CHARTING A ROADMAP TO GREAT IDEAS

A NEW APPROACH TO GROWTH

WHAT DO A REVOLUTIONARY scooter, cat food, and an eGovernance platform in Africa all have in common? More than you would think. They are all products of an innovation approach called the Jobs Roadmap. The Jobs Roadmap is a straightforward process that enables companies to consistently uncover new opportunities and generate great ideas. It's based on the groundbreaking work of Harvard Business School Professor Clayton Christensen, who popularized the concept of Jobs to be Done as a surefire way to spur innovation through looking not at what people happen to buy today, but rather at what are the underlying jobs they are trying to get done. By combining a deep understanding of customer needs, attitudes, and behaviors with hard data on the market landscape, the Jobs Roadmap enables companies to arrive at insights and solutions that are original and profitable. It makes the concept of Jobs to be Done highly actionable.

So much of today's current thinking sees innovation as a creative free-for-all where the best ideas inevitably rise to the surface. Teams sit in front of whiteboards and brainstorm lots and lots of ideas for new products that their company can offer, or they imagine numerous creative ways for their organization to grow. The winning ideas are usually chosen not through any consistent process but through a one-off assessment of what seems most promising given the information on hand, the company's internal climate, and the preferences of key stakeholders. Rarely are customer insights fed into the process in any meaningful and systematic way, and hardly ever do the results turn out to be breakthrough innovations. Even when organizations hit the jackpot with a new product or service, they soon realize that they don't know how to replicate their success.

This book was written to help organizations tackle the challenge of innovating in a way that is consistent and repeatable, using Jobs to be Done as the cornerstone of a rigorous framework. Our view is that to create innovation, it's necessary to focus as much on the approach taken as on the ideas themselves. In fact, we argue that getting the "how" of innovation right will in large part determine the quality of the "what"—the solutions that organizations ultimately produce. Through a detailed but straightforward approach, which we call the Jobs Roadmap, companies can navigate the various requirements of innovation and consistently come up with winning solutions.

Customer insight is at the center of the Jobs Roadmap. Understanding what jobs customers are trying to get done and the obstacles they face in doing so points to fertile terrain for new solutions. As a framework, the Jobs Roadmap offers a logical approach to any innovation project—enabling organizations to gain a deep understanding of their customers and key stakeholders, focusing idea generation on big opportunities and creating parameters that enable the quick and inexpensive testing of new solutions.

WHY WE NEED A NEW APPROACH

The customer is always right. Especially when it comes to innovation. Whether they know it or not, customers have the answers for where the next big breakthrough will be. The problem is that customers are notoriously bad at imagining the product that solves their problems and conceptualizing how they would interact with true breakthrough solutions. As Henry Ford reputedly put it, "If I'd asked people what they wanted, they would have said faster horses."[1] The trick is figuring out how to unlock the right information that can get you to the winning solution without relying solely on asking people what they want. This critical step is where many innovation efforts fail.

N
W
E
S
60°
70°

When the failures occur, it's not for a lack of effort. Companies often invest heavily to understand the so-called voice of the customer. They may gather overwhelming amounts of data around current and potential customer behavior, opinions, and attitudes. Problems arise when these organizations try to figure out what to do with all the information; they lack a structured way of determining what's important and what's not. This makes it difficult to figure out the right direction to take.

And that sad picture describes some of the more customer-centric organizations out there. More commonly, we find companies relying heavily on very short customer satisfaction surveys and highly circumscribed concept tests. These instruments have their place, but they offer little or no insight into the fundamental drivers of demand, what might cause customer preferences to shift, or where an industry should head. By looking with myopic intensity at data that is very easy to collect, companies can miss critical elements of the whole picture and cast their efforts in fundamentally wrong directions.

Even when it comes to new products, which seem straightforward to research, companies' track records are dire:

- More than 50 percent of newly launched products fall short of the company's projected expectations.
- Only 1 in 100 new products covers its development costs.
- Only 1 in 300 new products has a significant impact on customer purchase behavior, the product category, or the company's growth trajectory.[2]

Fortunately, the Jobs Roadmap provides a systematic way to beat the odds. Many new product failures can be avoided simply by understanding what jobs customers want to get done. Rather than leaping to foist a solution on the market, companies need to step back, listen to and observe real and potential customers (including how they react to early prototypes), and then hone in on strategic opportunity areas that show promise for growth.

DOING IT RIGHT

Making the innovation process work doesn't require flashes of genius, nor does it depend on glamorous ideas. By looking intently at customers in the strategic context of the company, great ideas can emerge from simple insights that are easy to act upon.

Consider the story of Uber, an on-demand car service that gets you an affordable ride within minutes. The idea isn't revolutionary. Taxis and car services have been around for a long time. In shaking up the taxi industry, part of what Uber brought to the table was a more cost-effective business model. By being a coordinator for drivers who had their own cars, Uber could substantially reduce its upfront costs by avoiding the need to pay for cars and medallions. But simply starting a price war by introducing a lower-cost model wouldn't have been enough to steer people away from traditional taxis. Large incumbents—even in relatively low-margin industries—usually have the resources to weather the storm, even if things are a bit uncomfortable for a while.

The key to Uber's success is that its efforts rely on Jobs-based principles. It's almost impossible to list all of the pain points associated with traditional taxis: Long waits while trying to find an empty cab, unfriendly drivers using every trick they know to drive up the fare, and "broken" credit card readers that force you to pay with cash are just a few of the difficulties. Uber's founders saw the problems that customers were facing and set out to offer a better alternative. Starting from the ground up, they produced a solution that would solve the most important jobs and alleviate as many frustrations as possible. The app's interface allows you to summon a car on demand and know exactly when it will arrive. The interface provides fare quotes in advance, and back-end staffers will refund fare overages when drivers take overly long routes. Every ride is charged to a credit card on file, eliminating the need to deal with cash. Beyond eliminating a number of important pain points, Uber focused on emotional jobs that the taxi industry had ignored, offering a sense of certainty and control that you simply don't have as you stand out in the cold waving at passing flashes of yellow or sit in the back of a cab endlessly watching the fare tick up on the meter. By focusing on fundamental jobs and taking a customer-centric perspective, Uber has grown to a $50 billion valuation in a little over five years.

WHAT LEADS COMPANIES ASTRAY

If the route to success is straightforward, why is it so uncommon? We offer five reasons why smart companies go astray.

First, doing things right requires a modest up-front investment of time. In typical corporate life, none of that is available. For example, Stephen, back in 1999, had the privilege of leading a team responsible for creating one of the first smartphones ever. Until he pushed back hard, he was given a whole two weeks from the project's inception to develop the specification for what would be in that device. Really.

Second, following the Jobs Roadmap entails asking difficult questions, many of which you'll struggle to answer. This is not the sort of behavior that's rewarded in most organizations. We are trained to be solution finders, from early schooling through to our annual employment reviews. Asking awkward questions can elicit equally awkward pauses, when people fumble for smart-sounding answers. You will need to get comfortable with the unknown. In tough questions lies great opportunity. Albert Einstein once said, "If I had an hour to solve a problem I'd spend 55 minutes thinking about the problem and five minutes thinking about solutions." Once you frame a problem very well, the answers can be rather obvious.

Third, market researchers and product developers can focus too heavily on the superficial questions—probing into whether customers like this or that better. They worry that if they delve too deeply into behavioral drivers, customers will come up with rationalizations that don't ultimately reflect their decision-making process when it comes time to make a purchase. A benefit of the Jobs Roadmap is that it allows you to target and understand discrete pieces of why customers act as they do, getting at the real root causes of behavior first and then becoming progressively more specific about the ramifications for the innovation.

Fourth, managers seek data to justify their conclusions, and data is rarely readily available about Jobs to be Done. Data can be produced reasonably quickly and inexpensively through primary research and test-and-learn experiments, but most companies still lack this information. This state of events is actually a good thing: It means that securing the data creates a true advantage for the company willing to do the work.

Last, and quite critically, we must discuss Clayton Christensen. As noted at the start of this introduction, Clay was the first person to popularize the notion of Jobs to be Done, although he is most famous for his concept of "disruptive innovation." Aside from Clay's remarkable brilliance, there is good reason why this one man, who mentored Stephen for many years, has produced these two concepts. The disruptive innovation theory holds, in part, that products starting out in small market niches can grow to upend industry giants. Companies already incumbent in an industry tend to ignore these niches, focusing on their business as they've traditionally defined it. For interlopers, though, looking at underlying jobs helps determine whether that niche is a dead end or a route to eventual greatness. By targeting an underaddressed job to be done, a disruptive entrant can attack incumbents in asymmetric fashion, building strength in corners of the market that seem uninteresting to the traditional giants. When the giants awaken, it is often too late to fight off the clever entrant. Disruption succeeds when it targets the right jobs to be done.

MAP OF THE BOOK

This book follows our Jobs Roadmap, which brings readers on a two-part journey to uncover and implement great ideas.

In Part I, "Understanding Jobs to be Done," we introduce readers to the concept of Jobs to be Done and help them construct their Jobs Atlas—a tool that systematically lays out customer insights relevant to the challenge being addressed. The Jobs Atlas has three subsections. The first, "Know Where You're Starting From," provides a process for discovering and prioritizing the jobs that customers are looking to get done, as well as identifying current customer approaches and pain points. The second subsection, "Chart the Destination and Roadblocks," helps the reader to define success from the customer's perspective while simultaneously determining what obstacles might stand in the way of buying or using a new solution. This information will be critical for translating Jobs-based insights into specific product features. The third subsection, "Make the Trip Worthwhile," integrates business model considerations into the process of exploring customer insights. This portion of the Jobs Atlas lets the reader determine what's at stake and figure out how to excel over competitors that the company may not have even recognized.

JOBS ROADMAP

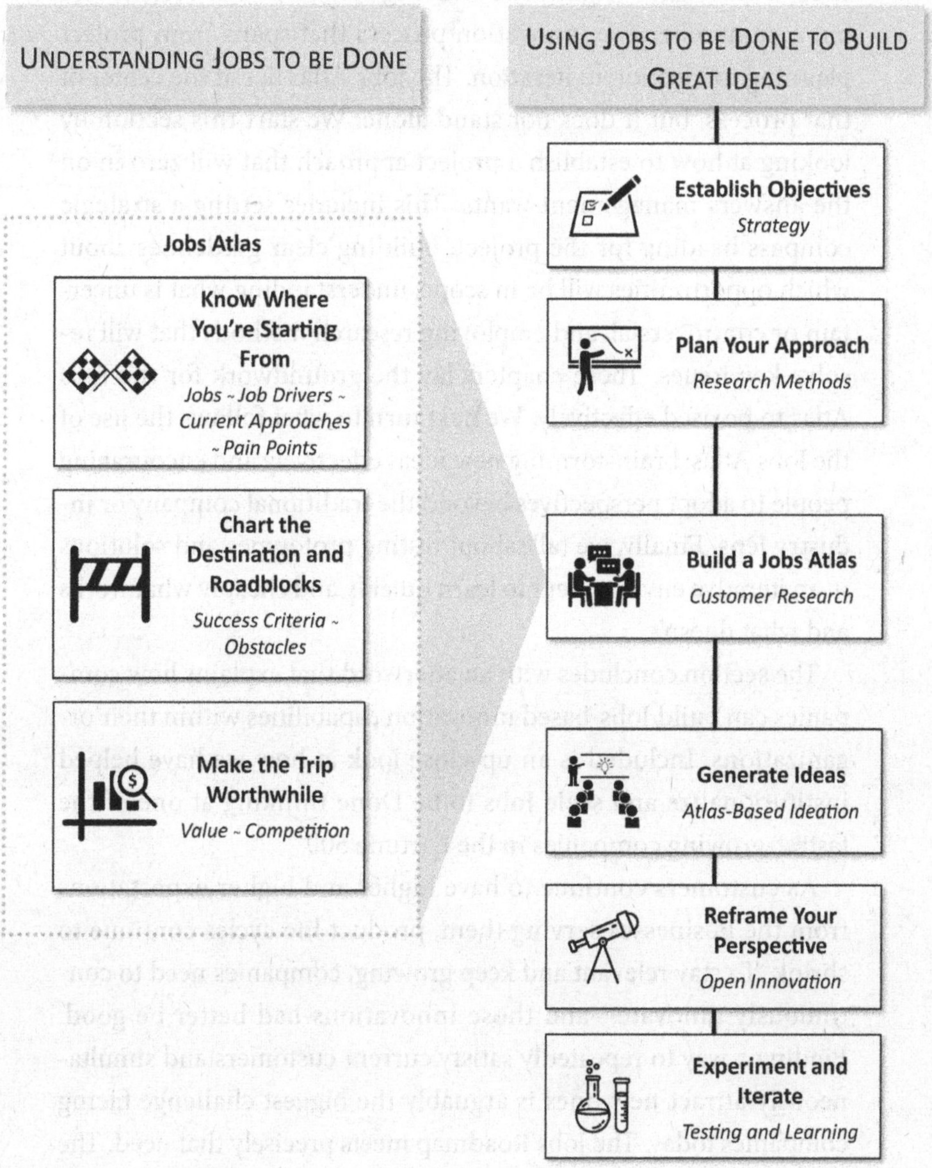

UNDERSTANDING JOBS TO BE DONE
USING JOBS TO BE DONE TO BUILD GREAT IDEAS
Jobs Atlas
Know Where You're Starting From
Jobs ~ Job Drivers ~ Current Approaches ~ Pain Points
Chart the Destination and Roadblocks
Success Criteria ~ Obstacles
Make the Trip Worthwhile
Value ~ Competition
Establish Objectives
Strategy
Plan Your Approach
Research Methods
Build a Jobs Atlas
Customer Research
Generate Ideas
Atlas-Based Ideation
Reframe Your Perspective
Open Innovation
Experiment and Iterate
Testing and Learning

Part II, *Using Jobs to be Done to Build Great Ideas*, explains how to turn customer insights into winning solutions. The section lays out a comprehensive innovation process that spans from project planning to ideation to iteration. The Jobs Atlas lies at the center of that process, but it does not stand alone. We start this section by looking at how to establish a project approach that will zero in on the answers management wants. This includes setting a strategic compass heading for the project, building clear guidelines about which opportunities will be in scope, understanding what is uncertain or controversial, and employing research methods that will resolve key issues. These chapters lay the groundwork for the Jobs Atlas to be used effectively. We next turn to what follows the use of the Jobs Atlas: brainstorming new ideas effectively and encouraging people to adopt perspectives beyond the traditional company or industry lens. Finally, we talk about testing prototypes and solutions in an iterative environment to learn quickly and cheaply what works and what doesn't.

The section concludes with an afterword that explains how companies can build Jobs-based innovation capabilities within their organizations. Included is an up-close look at how we have helped institutionalize and scale Jobs to be Done thinking at one of the fastest-growing companies in the Fortune 500.

As customers continue to have higher and higher expectations from the businesses serving them, product life cycles continue to shrink. To stay relevant and keep growing, companies need to continuously innovate—and those innovations had better be good. Finding a way to repeatedly satisfy current customers and simultaneously attract new ones is arguably the biggest challenge facing companies today. The Jobs Roadmap meets precisely that need. The chapters that follow provide a detailed explanation of not only how to gain deep customer insights but also how to turn those observations into breakthrough innovations. We have researched how some of the leading companies around the globe have used Jobs-based thinking to create successful and lasting new product lines, and we have combined that with our years of experience in helping companies put the Jobs methods to the test in their own industries. As you read on, you will learn how these lessons can help create success in the face of your own current challenges.

PART I

UNDERSTANDING JOBS TO BE DONE

FINDING HIGH-POTENTIAL AVENUES FOR GROWTH

It's not enough to have a strong vision or a single great idea. To successfully innovate—in a way that doesn't mimic every other competitor—you need to see the range of opportunities open to you. A serious customer-centric view of the landscape will tell you what routes contain latent opportunities for you to exploit. It can also lead you away from uncomfortable pain points associated with current approaches and guide you through the pitfalls of getting customers to act in unfamiliar ways. Importantly, a true customer-centric approach will pinpoint the ways in which a new solution has to excel over existing offerings and lead you down the right paths to making money.

THE CENTRAL ROLE OF JOBS TO BE DONE

All over the world, people go about their days getting things done. Much of what they do is aimed at satisfying a collection of short- and long-term objectives that they see as being related to their well-being. The many decisions that they make throughout the day—which toothpaste to use, whether to drink coffee or tea, what product to buy for their company—are all part of satisfying these objectives, as each person defines them.

But what if people know only part of what they want? Or—even more radical—what if they don't really understand why they want what they want? While such confusion at first glance seems like a recipe for innovation disaster, it is precisely in this knowledge gap where opportunities for new growth exist. Throughout this section, we will answer such questions as: How can companies use this knowledge gap to attract new customers or launch new products? How can figuring out the known and unknown drivers of consumer behavior give companies an advantage in the marketplace? And if people themselves don't know what they want or why they want it, how can someone else figure it out?

Just because everyone dreams of a new car, it doesn't mean everyone is dreaming of the same new car.

This process for finding growth opportunities is the product of 12 years of our own research and experimentation, which builds on further precedent before then. The core premise is the intuitive but not so obvious idea that by digging into the "why" of people's actions, you can uncover the set of reasons—emotional, psychological, and practical—that drive people to behave in certain ways rather than in others. Ultimately, people are just trying to get things done in their lives, whether they are making a purchase for their own use, collaborating in a business-to-business transaction, or consuming a government service. They can employ a wide range of solutions to get these jobs done, so concentrating attention on solutions used—as marketers typically do—is incorrect. It is the jobs that really matter. Once you understand what jobs people are striving to do, it becomes easier to predict what products or services they will take up and which will fall flat.

While not the only requirement for successfully innovating or growing, identifying the range of jobs that current or future customers are trying to satisfy is central to any innovation strategy; it guards against pursuing phantom opportunities and grounds the innovation in smart data. The Jobs to be Done approach—which is explained in detail in this section—creates a powerful method for creating breakthrough innovations again and again.

GETTING RESULTS

The Jobs to be Done framework succeeds because it focuses innovators on the right questions rather than having them jump directly to devising solutions. This can be counterintuitive. After all, countless stories celebrating genius emphasize the moment of problem-solving insight. But it is actually the framing of problems that often leads to breakthrough ideas. Companies can waste thousands of hours and risk undertaking bad projects because they miss the critical—and often underappreciated—step of laying out very clear and rigorously defined problem statements.

Breakthroughs come from reimagining problems, not from creating an incrementally better solution to a well-understood challenge.

To help people look at their challenges in a different way, we tell them to dig into the underlying "why" of consumer behavior and not just focus on the "what." For instance, parents may choose to bring their children to a movie on a Saturday afternoon, but the underlying job is to keep the kids entertained. A movie is just one possible way of satisfying that job. Job drivers—the underlying context that makes certain jobs more or less important—will influence customers' choices in how they satisfy a job. In the movie example, the age of the children or the weather that day might make a difference in how the job of entertaining children is satisfied. The movie theater's true competition is not merely other cinemas but also playgrounds, arcades, and other diversions. While offering a discount on ticket prices or a better array of snacks might help compete against the cinema across town, these solutions ultimately represent a superficial way of thinking about competition. A better way to win might be to set up a small indoor playground or to offer a space for socializing with dates after a movie ends. By understanding the real motivators of behavior, a company can uncover new markets and previously ignored levers of innovation at its disposal.

MAP OF THE SECTION

This section of the book shows how to construct the Jobs Atlas—the overall look at the landscape that is a prerequisite to plotting routes to any specific solution and indeed may reveal destinations you have previously overlooked. Chapters 1 through 3 provide the tools for understanding what jobs your customers are looking to get done, why they prioritize some jobs over others, and what pain points prevent them from being satisfied with the solutions they currently use. Chapters 4 and 5 build on today's landscape to explore how to create solutions that correspond to a customer-generated definition

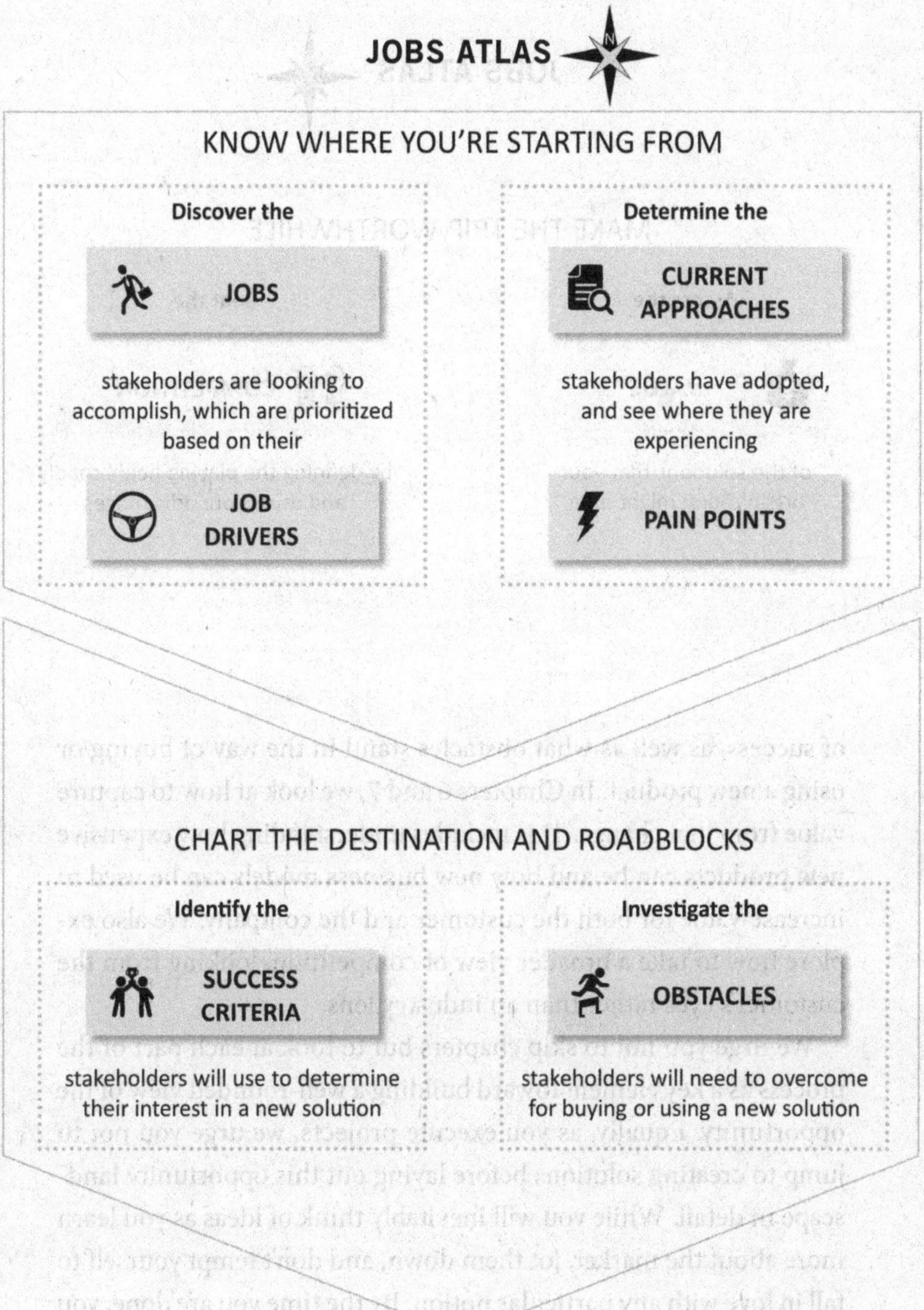
JOBS ATLAS
N
KNOW WHERE YOU'RE STARTING FROM
Discover the
JOBS
stakeholders are looking to accomplish, which are prioritized based on their
JOB DRIVERS
Determine the
CURRENT APPROACHES
stakeholders have adopted, and see where they are experiencing
PAIN POINTS
CHART THE DESTINATION AND ROADBLOCKS
Identify the
SUCCESS CRITERIA
stakeholders will use to determine their interest in a new solution
Investigate the
OBSTACLES
stakeholders will need to overcome for buying or using a new solution

illustration continues

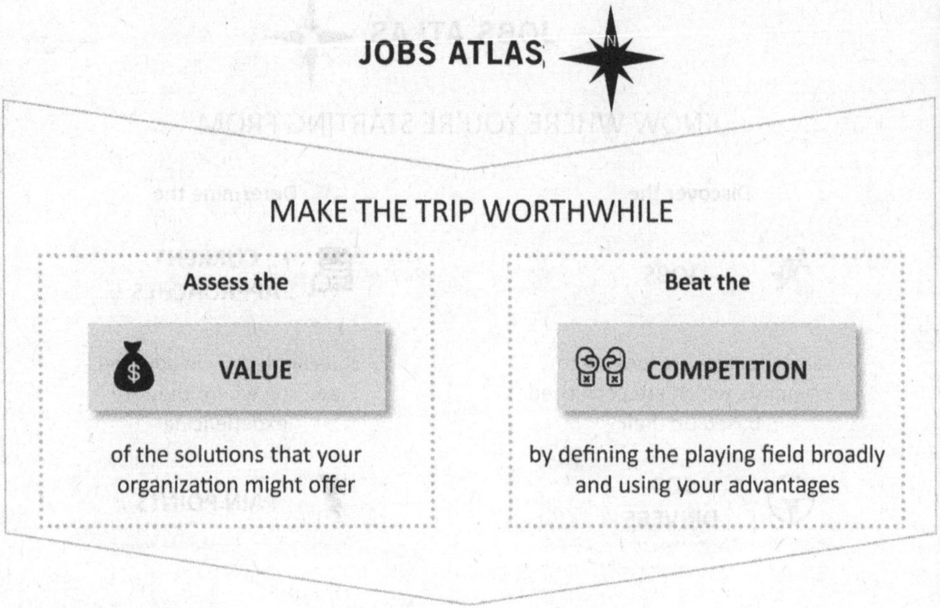
JOBS ATLAS
N
MAKE THE TRIP WORTHWHILE
Assess the
VALUE
of the solutions that your organization might offer
Beat the
COMPETITION
by defining the playing field broadly and using your advantages

of success, as well as what obstacles stand in the way of buying or using a new product. In Chapters 6 and 7, we look at how to capture value from that change. This includes understanding how expensive new products can be and how new business models can be used to increase value for both the customer and the company. We also explore how to take a broader view of competition, looking from the customer's eyes rather than an industry lens.

We urge you not to skip chapters but to look at each part of the process as a key element toward building a well-rounded view of the opportunity. Equally, as you execute projects, we urge you not to jump to creating solutions before laying out this opportunity landscape in detail. While you will inevitably think of ideas as you learn more about the market, jot them down, and don't tempt yourself to fall in love with any particular notion. By the time you are done, you should have an abundant array of solutions stemming from a full understanding of the landscape. They may even appear obvious to you, until you realize that you didn't have these ideas before you started the process.

KNOW WHERE YOU'RE STARTING FROM

Discover the

JOBS

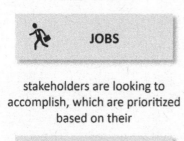

stakeholders are looking to accomplish, which are prioritized based on their

JOB DRIVERS

Determine the

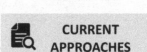

CURRENT APPROACHES

stakeholders have adopted, and see where they are experiencing

PAIN POINTS

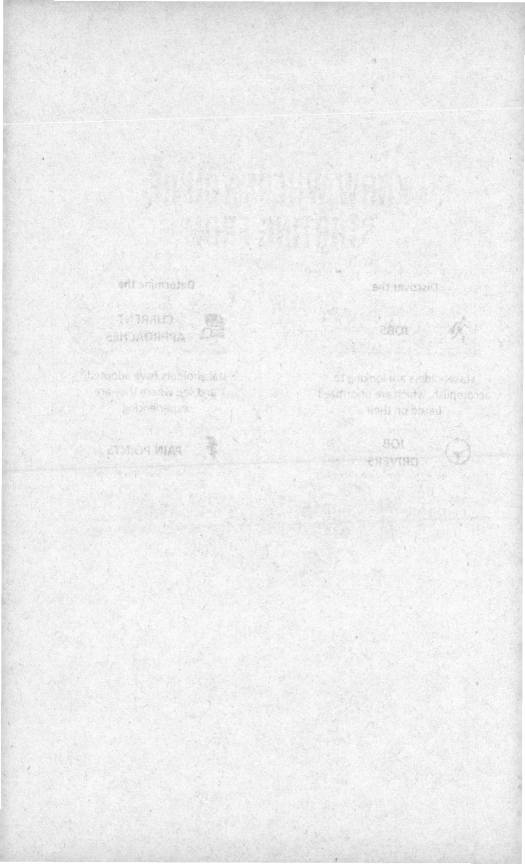

1

JOBS

WHAT CUSTOMERS ARE TRYING TO GET DONE

IN THE LATE 1990s, Stephen led one of the world's first smartphone development projects. His team at Psion PLC combined the innards of the Personal Digital Assistant (PDA), which Psion had originally invented in the 1980s, with telephony components from Motorola to create a device with a long list of features. The team was incredibly excited about all of the things the new device could do. You could even send a fax from your phone! But customers were confused, the technical complexity was overwhelming, and the device was quite costly.

Around the same time, a Canadian company called Research in Motion was taking a different approach, focusing on a simple hierarchy of jobs that people wanted to get done with a smartphone. Their product—the Blackberry—did far fewer things and was much less stylish. But it dominated the field for the next seven years—an eon in that industry.

The key to the Blackberry's success wasn't great technology or clever advertisements. It wasn't about getting the priorities of the

Throwing in everything but the kitchen sink—then adding the kitchen sink—makes your product bloated, not better.

customer right; Stephen's team had been diligent about asking people what they wanted ("Maps!" "Games!"). Rather, the Research in Motion effort triumphed because it looked at customers the right way, focusing on a single critical job to be done: keeping in touch through email.

Jobs help you to focus on what really matters, rather than trying to add on cool features that muddle the customer experience and make the product less compelling. It is a concept that Stephen really wished he had known about when he designed that device.

IN THIS CHAPTER, YOU WILL LEARN:

- Why to focus on jobs over past purchase behavior.
- How to win on both the functional and emotional levels.
- How understanding jobs can lead to the better design of products, services, and business models.

USING JOBS TO REDEFINE MARKETS AND CREATE OPPORTUNITIES

When thinking about how to launch a new product or bring in new customers, too many companies focus on what people are currently buying. They use existing purchase data to define their markets quite narrowly. They begin to think of themselves as booksellers and PC companies. Then when sales dip or management makes aggressive growth demands, they end up asking the wrong questions. How can we sell more books? How can we build a better PC? This tunnel-visioned approach to market definition creates a very small solution space, and it can blind companies to threats from untraditional sources.

Customers' jobs exist independently from what people are buying, making it essential to see the world from the customer's perspective rather than from the vantage of a company that happens to be selling something. As the late Harvard Business School Professor Theodore Levitt famously told his students, "People don't want to buy a quarter-inch drill. They want a quarter-inch hole."

Snapchat gives us a good example of a company that has eschewed industry trends in favor of a customer-centric perspective. Snapchat is particularly interesting because it shows how a company is attracting the notoriously fickle millennial demographic to steal market share in the social media/mobile messaging sphere—an arena that's barely old enough to be disrupted. To a casual observer familiar with the general direction of the industry, Snapchat shouldn't be successful. While Facebook is focusing on delivering enhanced search functionality that allows you to find fond memories among old posts, the ephemeral nature of Snapchat's messages makes that impossible. Instagram continues to add new filters and photo-editing capabilities, but Snapchat offers just a handful of filters and tools that are on par with the earliest versions of Microsoft Paint. Twitter opened a world where you can follow the musings of virtually anyone, yet Snapchat restricts you to the posts of added friends and a few preselected organizations.

Despite its apparent inferiority, Snapchat has already grown to reach 6 billion video views per day (just trailing Facebook's 8 billion), and it has a valuation of $16 billion.[1] So what explains Snapchat's success? Rather than cramming its app with all of the features of its closest competitors, Snapchat has focused on satisfying a handful of emotional jobs that are important to its target users. Other social media apps have been criticized for creating an atmosphere of yearning in which users are bombarded with images of fun adventures and expensive vacations. Instead, Snapchat offers a way to document something closer to real life, allowing users to share moments and feelings without an expectation that their posts will be glamorous or that they'll look their best. Framed in this light, the lack of a "Like" button, the inability to search old photos, and the lack of ways to enhance what you're sharing all become advantages rather than drawbacks. Importantly for the company's target demographic, Snapchat also lets users feel like they're part of a chosen community that they helped build. With a younger user base and the ability to share with only selected friends, Snapchat offers a way for millennials to engage with a platform that isn't shared with their parents, extended family members, and employers. Snapchat isn't for everyone, and it doesn't try to be. Instead, its founders resisted the temptation to copy the competition, building an app that helps an identifiable user base satisfy a handful of important jobs really well.

WINNING ON THE FUNCTIONAL AND EMOTIONAL LEVELS

Customers have jobs that are both functional and emotional in nature, and companies need to design offerings that win on both levels. First consider the functional jobs. Although these can be more straightforward to satisfy than emotional ones, many companies get so excited about adding new functionality that they overlook the underlying jobs. In general, satisfying a customer's functional jobs requires pulling three levers: focusing on real jobs, satisfying those jobs for particular customers or occasions, and designing solutions that prioritize jobs over features.

Critically, it is important to satisfy real jobs. Although this sounds simple, too many companies start with a new idea and then hope that people will realize its inherent appeal. The end result is often a product that solves low-priority jobs or jobs that people don't really have. Reading glasses, for example, were a great idea. Yet for several hundred years after their invention in the thirteenth century, there was virtually no demand for them. Because there was little need to read things up close, most farsighted people didn't even realize they were farsighted. It wasn't until the mid-fifteenth century, when Gutenberg's printing press catalyzed the widespread printing of books, that people began seeking out a way to ease the strain as they tried to read.[2] Once reading books became a high-priority job, demand for curing farsightedness soared.

Jobs are different from success criteria or metrics that determine whether a job has been achieved. Brookwood, an independent school for young children in Massachusetts that we've worked with, used to advertise itself to prospective parents as a "community of exuberant learners." That phrasing was evocative, but unfortunately it placed a lot of emphasis on the idea of community. Finding a community for their children was not a job many parents rated as important, and there were many other ways to accomplish that objective such as soccer teams and neighborhood organizations. Community was, however, a means of determining whether children felt comfortable learning and were valued for their individual personalities and talents, not just for their test scores. As part of its rebranding efforts, Brookwood has reframed its messaging around real jobs to be done in order to drive an increase in applications.

Propositions also need to be designed with particular customers and occasions in mind. Designing for some theoretical average user can undermine the potential gains you may get from understanding distinct types of customers' jobs to be done. When we introduce the Jobs concept to new audiences, we sometimes run a mock focus group, pretending that we're working for an ice cream company. At first, we tell people we need to sell more ice cream. They usually think about customers on average and respond that we need more flavors, more sales outlets, fewer calories, and lower prices. That's not very practical, nor does it respond directly to jobs to be done. So we then ask people a different question: Thinking about the last time that you had ice cream, why did you do that, and if you hadn't had ice cream, what would you have done otherwise? The answers are *completely* different. People were celebrating an occasion, and they decided to have ice cream to spend more time together after dinner. They were trying to cool down at the beach, and ice cream competed against water. They were taking a stroll and saw a new shop, and they wanted a new experience rather than just following an old routine. Focusing on particular people in specific contexts creates far richer and more useful detail than thinking about things on average.

Once you have identified a few high-priority jobs, it is important to make sure that you satisfy those jobs well. Companies often spread their resources too thinly, adding extra features that sound good in advertisements. Yet those features rarely drive decision making. Microsoft can boast that upgrading to Excel 2007 increased the limit on unique colors per workbook from 56 to 4.3 billion, but will that really matter? Even worse, the payoff from new features is often short-lived, inasmuch as features generally prove easy for competitors to replicate. Why couldn't Excel boast a template that helps people balance their checkbooks? That's a job that, according to our research, a significant proportion of banking customers accomplish using Excel, but in a currently awkward and error-prone way.

Focusing on features makes you lose sight of important jobs. As the mobility trend further embedded itself in the PC world, Blackberry rushed to get on the tablet train. It quickly got out the PlayBook, which had a touch screen and an icon-based display. It boasted a great list of features and was actually quite slick in a number of ways. On the other hand, the PlayBook failed to take advantage of the company's biggest strength: It launched without native email support! In doing so, the PlayBook glossed over key mobile communication jobs just so that Blackberry could have a competing tablet in the marketplace.

As much as companies may struggle with functional jobs, they typically get more attention than emotional jobs. Emotional jobs tend to be neglected in business, especially outside the realm of consumer packaged goods such as food and cleaning products. Emotional jobs can be difficult to articulate, and solution-oriented managers have a hard time dwelling on how their products can satisfy emotional jobs. Enterprise software companies, for instance, are fond of saying how their worlds are intensely rational, and then they struggle to explain why great products are never broadly adopted or why companies stick with long-term vendors even though their offerings are outmoded. As competitors find ways to satisfy the same functional jobs at a lower price point, emotional elements can provide a vital way to differentiate your product.

Sennheiser, Bose, and JBL have figured out how to make high-quality audio products. When Apple paid $3.2 billion to buy Beats Electronics in 2014, countless critics and music enthusiasts came out ranting about the inferior quality of Beats' headphones.[3] But despite competing against technically superior products, Beats had a 40 percent market share four years after entering the market. So why are people so excited about Beats? The company hits on emotional jobs. Put simply, the $300 price tag for a set of Beats headphones is the cost of a seat at the lunchroom's cool table. From the beginning, Beats focused on getting its headphones into as many music videos, locker rooms, and runway shoots as possible, ensuring that they were associated with celebrity glamor and status. Going a step further, Beats offers a wealth of limited editions for movies and sports leagues, creating more opportunities for users to stand out and express themselves. Although the headphones have to perform at a certain functional threshold, their ability to satisfy emotional jobs allows them to command a premium in the market. Much like Beats, companies with products that excel along emotional dimensions can stand out even as the competition becomes more and more commoditized.

USING JOBS TO DESIGN BETTER SOLUTIONS

Doing research to uncover customers' jobs to be done will undoubtedly leave you with a long list of jobs. Much like the problem of adding too many features, attempting to satisfy too many jobs leaves you with a complicated, expensive, one-size-fits-none product. You

THE JOBS TO BE DONE DIFFERENCE

Today's marketers are bombarded with directives about what to look for when gathering customer insights. Sorting through all the jargon can be almost as challenging as actually designing a new product. Here's a quick look at how jobs are fundamentally different.

Jobs are...

- The underlying tasks that customers are trying to get done
- Customer demands that are specific to discrete customer types and occasions
- Actionable statements that guide the design of new solutions

Jobs are not...

- **Needs – customer articulations of what they would like to see in a new product**

  Jobs are real representations of what customers are trying to get done, even if customers cannot articulate what they want or do not understand the range of possibilities for a breakthrough innovation.
- **Need states – occasion-based statements about what customers want and how they want to get it**

  While the Jobs framework also takes an occasion-based lens, the focus is on fundamental tasks. The framework allows for tailored solutions that can satisfy multiple jobs, including in ways that customers have not yet thought about.
- **Outcomes – measurable goals that customers are seeking to meet**

  While customer-created success criteria are useful, jobs are more fundamental. Because customers are notoriously bad at stipulating the emotional outcomes they want to achieve and providing outcome-driven guidance on products that do not yet exist, it is more useful to understand what those customers are trying to get done.
- **Attributes – features that add value to a new solution**

  Jobs are not simply easily replicable features that can be used to promote a product. They address underlying customer concerns, allowing for a broader solution space in which new offerings can take a wider variety of forms.

end up with the fax-sending smartphone described at the start of this chapter. Designing a breakthrough product requires making difficult decisions and trade-offs. At its core, your new solution will need to focus on satisfying a handful of key jobs. The sweet spot lies with jobs that are important yet undersatisfied in the eyes of the customer. These jobs will act as your North Star, guiding the rest of the decisions you make when designing the new offering. Then, at a lower level, you can focus on satisfying secondary jobs that allow you to differentiate your product further, as well as on table-stakes jobs that have to be accomplished by any product in the class.

To see how this works in practice, let's journey to the small town of Ipswich, Massachusetts. Sitting about 30 miles northeast of Boston, Ipswich is a coastal community with a rich colonial history. The town was founded in 1634, and many of the homes are quite old. In fact, the town boasts more homes built before 1725 than any other place in the United States.[4] First Ipswich Bank, much like its competitors in the area, offers the standard range of fixed-rate, adjustable-rate, and jumbo mortgages for the owners of such houses. While all of the banks in the area are rolling out innovative solutions, such as mobile banking options, their mortgage products are hardly exciting. Most banks fail to recognize that the customer's job is not to complete a mortgage transaction but to move into a new home. That is the real North Star for the customer's journey, and understanding this reveals many aspects that are undershot by existing offerings. First Ipswich seems to get this. For those buying a home built before 1750, the bank offers a unique mortgage that allows customers to add on to the initial loan amount to cover the additional renovation expenses that commonly arise when dealing with old houses. If you find out that you have to install new plumbing, for example, you can roll that cost into your mortgage rather than having to take out a second mortgage for the effort. That is Jobs-based thinking at work.

THIS CHAPTER IN PRACTICE— USING JOBS TO APPEAL TO NEW CUSTOMERS

Yowzit had concerns about its website. This South African Internet start-up, which runs a leading site for customers to rate and review a wide range of services, was doing well but not experiencing exponential growth. Management wanted to connect with customers in an intuitive way, driving further traffic and longer visits to the site. As the company's managing director, Pramod Mohanlal, put it, "We knew that we were addressing a part of an important job, but we needed to understand more deeply what context we could fit into."

The company started talking in depth to its users. It didn't ask initially for specific ideas for improvement but rather tried to understand key jobs in certain contexts. When were the last three times you used the site? Why did you do that? If you hadn't used the site, what would you have done? How did using the site make you feel? What feelings were important to you then? How did the site's use fit into the broader set of things you were trying to accomplish?

Using this approach, the company thought up new tools for its customers to use and figured out how to position the site in a Jobs-focused way. In addition to promoting functional benefits, such as tools focused on just-in-time ways to improve a night out, the company created ways to satisfy emotional jobs, including new branding around self-expression. It also added new features such as video reviews that enabled in-the-moment expressiveness, particularly for users who felt uncomfortable writing on the fly. The company has used these insights not only to drive much greater traffic but also to drive entry into new spheres such as rating public services. Mohanlal explained: "Thinking about jobs made us recognize that we were playing at the edge of a huge market, and we've vastly expanded our potential by keying into what really motivates behavior."

CHAPTER SUMMARY

Many companies try to innovate by looking backward. They focus on what they are already selling or doing and on how their customers currently behave. By focusing on jobs, you look deeper—at what really drives behavior. This perspective can totally change the innovation landscape, and it ensures that ideas connect with customers' true motivations rather than with what they happen to be doing today. A Jobs approach sets you up to win both today and into the future.

Focusing on Jobs to be Done, rather than on past customer purchase behavior, allows you to define a broader solution space with more opportunities for innovation.

Designing a product that satisfies functional jobs in a superior way is a necessary first step. If you also appeal to customers' emotional needs, whether your customer is an individual consumer or a large corporation, you can make your product a breakthrough success. This requires designing offerings for specific customers on specific occasions.

Be wary of getting into feature wars with your competitors. Features are easy to copy, and adding too many can ultimately make for a frustrating user experience. Similarly, focus on satisfying high-priority jobs, looking first to the jobs that are both important and undersatisfied in the eyes of the customer.

2

JOB DRIVERS

WHY CUSTOMERS HAVE DIFFERENT JOBS

IN THE MID TO late 2000s, online retailers were driving down prices on consumer electronics. As competition increased and margins thinned, Circuit City tried a number of tactics to weather the storm. It narrowed its product selection, made its stores look like those of its more successful competitors, and trimmed personnel costs. Nothing worked. In 2009, Circuit City closed all of its remaining stores. Around the same time and facing similar pressures, Best Buy tried a different approach. It created a fresh customer segmentation that was unlike the demographic-driven segmentations that tended to dominate the retail industry. It unveiled a set of new personas—including Buzz (the young tech enthusiast) and Jill (the suburban soccer mom)—that wrapped together demographics, lifestyle factors, and other insights into customers' everyday lives. The company embraced Jobs to be Done as a part of this process.

Armed with its new segmentation, Best Buy funded a $50 million pilot renovation program to redesign 110 of its stores in order to cater to the customer types that most frequently shopped there. So, for example, products that Jill might be interested in were put on lower shelves so that she could get a closer look at them. The sales staff was trained about what else Jill might have going on in her life, making it easier to cross-sell relevant products. Stores that were redesigned to fit the needs of its major customer segments reported same-store sales growth of over 9 percent—double that of the stores that had not been redesigned.[1]

While jobs are the tasks that customers are looking to get done in their lives, job drivers are the underlying contextual elements that make certain jobs more or less important. Jill's contextual job drivers—the three children who need to get to trombone lessons, soccer practice, and a dance recital in different parts of town—make certain jobs like speedy meal preparation and adequate nutrition rise to the top. So when Jill stops at a Best Buy to research microwaves, she's not going to be upsold on an oven. She might, however, be interested in learning about other smart appliances that offer the speed of a microwave with a cooking technique that does a better job of locking in a meal's nutrients. By knowing why people have distinct jobs, we can target segments of customers in ways that intuitively make sense to them.

IN THIS CHAPTER, YOU WILL LEARN:

- What categories job drivers fall into.
- How job drivers combine with jobs to create meaningful customer segments.

WHERE JOB DRIVERS COME FROM

Job drivers come in three flavors: attitudes, background, and circumstances (see Figure 2-1).

To help understand the differences among these three categories, let's talk about Stan, who is shopping for a new car. Like other car

CATEGORIES OF JOB DRIVERS

TYPE	DEFINITION	EXAMPLES
Attitudes	Personality traits that affect behavior and decision making	• Social pressures • Personality • Expectations of others
Background	Long-term context that affects behavior and decision making	• Geographic / cultural dynamics • Family dynamics • Socioeconomic status
Circumstances	Immediate or near-term factors that affect behavior and decision making	• Weather / environmental factors • Work schedule • Unexpected events

Figure 2-1

buyers, Stan has certain key jobs to be done, such as avoiding breakdowns, having a comfortable ride, and ensuring his personal safety. It seems settled. Stan should get a Toyota Camry. They are reliable, sufficiently comfortable, and safe. How could he go wrong with one of the top-selling cars in America?

Stan's attitudes—his social or personality-based job drivers—begin to differentiate him from other car buyers, causing a shift in which jobs are more or less important. As it turns out, Stan has an MBA from a prestigious school. Many of his peers and colleagues are wildly successful. These factors drive Stan to show off his own level of success. Not a problem. We can put Stan in a Mercedes-Benz S-Class, a top-of-the-line luxury sedan. It satisfies the same primary jobs as the Camry but also allows Stan to display his wealth. Saving money is a less important job for Stan, given his earning prospects, so the Mercedes it is.

As it turns out, Stan's background—his long-term job drivers—will also play a role. Stan lives in New England at the top of a steep hill. These geographical factors drive Stan's need for a more powerful car that can get him up the hill during the snowy winter months. The Mercedes will not do after all. Maybe the Porsche Cayenne SUV would be a better fit for Stan. With its advanced traction capabilities, the Cayenne satisfies Stan's needs for power. Looking at the reviews, the Cayenne is less reliable over the long term than the Camry, but Stan gets a new car every few years anyway. His emphasis is on short-term reliability, so a new Cayenne should pose no problem.

There is a final twist in the story, though. Stan's circumstances—his immediate or near-term job drivers—make the Cayenne impractical. Stan happens to be shopping for a car during lacrosse season. This year, Stan volunteered to coach his son's lacrosse team, and he is worried that he may have to haul some gear in the back of his car. The Cayenne may not have the cargo room. Ultimately, Stan decides on a larger luxury SUV, the Cadillac Escalade.

What Stan's story tells us is that even customers who have similar jobs will make different decisions about what products they use to satisfy those jobs. The Camry buyer and the Escalade buyer may both care about safety, reliability, and cargo space, but their job drivers cause them to define those terms differently and place more emphasis on one set of jobs over the other. The job drivers are facts, such as Stan's pedigree. They are not jobs themselves, but they have a big impact on which jobs are important. At the same time, job drivers can cause entirely new jobs to matter, such as Stan's need to

STAN'S JOBS AND JOB DRIVERS

	JOB DRIVERS	AFFECTED JOBS
Attitudes	• High educational background • Successful peer group	• Show off success
Background	• Location of his home (New England / hill) • Wealth / car purchase frequency	• Climb hills • Hold up over long term
Circumstances	• Volunteer activities as a coach	• Transport cargo

Figure 2-2

show off. Ultimately, it is a combination of jobs and job drivers that differentiates customers (see Figure 2-2).

USING JOB DRIVERS TO SEGMENT CUSTOMERS

Good marketing revolves around customer segmentation. Not all products are well suited for all customers, so defining distinct segments of customers enables marketers to target certain products at particular segments. Then there can be a good fit between what is offered and who is buying it.

A customer segment—whether it consists of your customers, competitors' customers, noncustomers, or a mix of the three—has a degree of homogeneity in what it needs and how it buys and consumes. The more that a segmentation has to cover all aspects of a customer's experience—from how she gains awareness about a product to where she buys it to what she wants to choose—the less focused it will be. Sometimes segments do not need to encompass such diverse territory. A product development team, for instance, may care deeply about what customers are trying to get done, but they are not concerned with how customers view advertising to find out about new offerings. The company can address that challenge later. For now, the team just wants to segment customers by how they consider and use products.

Jobs and job drivers are critical factors for segmentation (see Figure 2-3). Whereas many (poor) segmentation schemes focus on who people are or how they are behaving, jobs and job drivers explain why they are acting a certain way and how they might consider new offerings. In a public sector context, they explain why people want certain benefits and why they prioritize things as they do. Without knowing the "why," facts are sterile. For example, a credit card company we worked with once segmented its customers based on life stage, which seemingly made sense, except that life stages had almost no correlation to card spending, use of revolving credit, and other key metrics. So it then segmented customers based on their card spending or revolving, which did tell the company about who is profitable but explained nothing about why these people acted as they did. A deeper look revealed that there are several distinct types of high-spending customers, such as people who consume a lot, business travelers, and small-business owners. These individuals have entirely different job drivers, and it was folly to lump them together

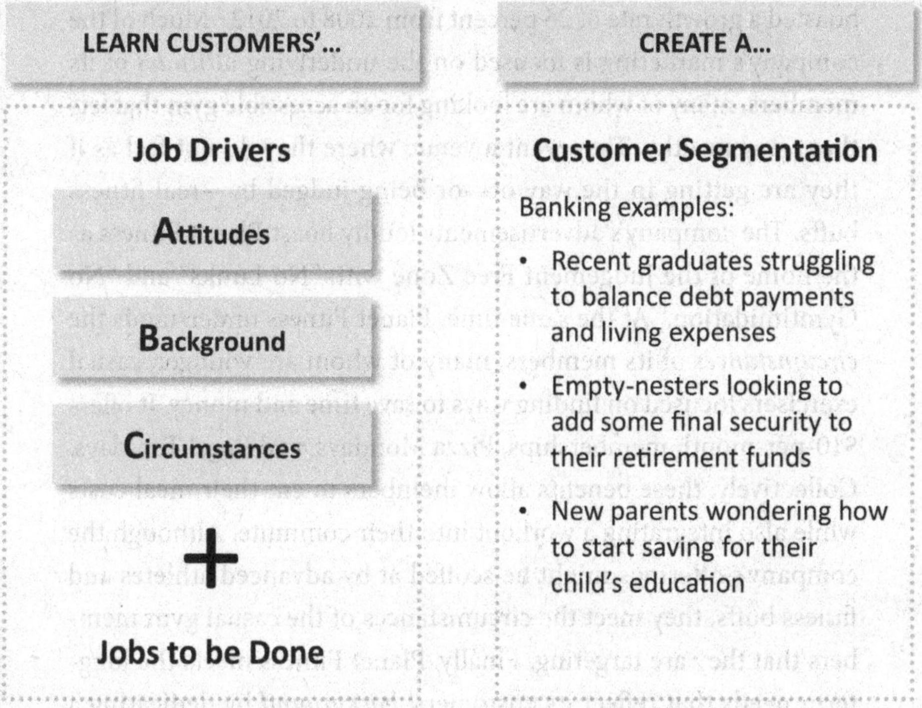
LEARN CUSTOMERS'...
CREATE A...
Job Drivers
Attitudes
Background
Circumstances
+
Jobs to be Done
Customer Segmentation
Banking examples:
Recent graduates struggling to balance debt payments and living expenses
Empty-nesters looking to add some final security to their retirement funds
New parents wondering how to start saving for their child's education

Figure 2-3

into a one-size-fits-none segment of high spenders. Knowing that high-spending cardholders were between the ages of 35 and 50 and had large incomes was nice, but knowing that the reason some spend so much was because they travel on business at least once per month yielded a trove of opportunities for the company.

Gyms also illustrate how the distinct categories of job drivers can factor into segmentation. In the past, many gyms attempted to distinguish themselves based on features. They would look at factors such as season, location, member age, and member gender to determine whether to promote perks such as free tanning or on-site juice bars. More recently, however, gyms are being built and marketed around underlying jobs and job drivers. Take Planet Fitness, which ranked third on the 2014 Forbes list of America's best franchises and boasted a growth rate of 26 percent from 2008 to 2012.[2] Much of the company's marketing is focused on the underlying *attitudes* of its members, many of whom are looking for an accessible gym that lets them stay healthy. They want a venue where they do not feel as if they are getting in the way of—or being judged by—real fitness buffs. The company's advertisements loudly boast Planet Fitness as the home of the Judgement Free Zone with "No Lunks" and "No Gymtimidation." At the same time, Planet Fitness understands the *circumstances* of its members, many of whom are younger, casual exercisers focused on finding ways to save time and money. It offers $10-per-month memberships, Pizza Mondays, and Bagel Tuesdays. Collectively, these benefits allow members to cut their meal costs while also integrating a workout into their commute. Although the company's offerings might be scoffed at by advanced athletes and fitness buffs, they meet the circumstances of the casual gym members that they are targeting. Finally, Planet Fitness meets the long-term needs that reflect its customers' *background* by dedicating a high percentage of its space to cardio and strength-training machines that emphasize easy-to-attain everyday fitness. Although some athletes need access to full-size pools and free weights to meet strict training goals, most casual gym members prefer a more accessible gym experience.

A strict demographic segmentation never would have illuminated the need for the Planet Fitness model. Similarly, companies that segment based solely on customers' jobs may also miss a key piece of the puzzle. Trying to distinguish customers based simply on their jobs tends to result in customer segments that are impractical. Often, a few key jobs will be almost universally important. Going back to our car purchase example, it's rational for everyone to say that being able to stop a car in a short distance is an important job. In reality, however, most people aren't going to purchase a car because of the quality of the brakes.

Where's the smoothie BAR?!

On the other hand, looking at a mix of jobs and job drivers begins to create a clearer picture of how various customer types are distinct. Imagine a couple with a newborn baby. While other customers may say that safety is important, it is likely much more front and center for this couple. At the end of the day, safety—including the ability to stop quickly—may be more of a deciding factor for them. At the same time, the number of children they have may raise or lower the importance they place on having adequate room to transport cargo. On a more emotional level, their attitudes may also play a major role in the decision-making process. Maybe they just do not see themselves as minivan people. They are already accepting that a new child will require them to make a number of lifestyle trade-offs, so perhaps the new car is an opportunity to cling to a vestige of whimsical fun. Ultimately, each customer type will have a unique combination of jobs and drivers of varying importance that lead them to their buying decisions. A segmentation built on jobs and job drivers will help to group these customers together, creating valuable insights into how prevalent a particular customer type is and what customers might eventually be willing to buy.

THIS CHAPTER IN PRACTICE—SEGMENTING THE MARKET

An education provider came to us a few years back looking to assess potential opportunities in providing quality online degrees to people who wanted to obtain them as fast as possible. Although the company had heard much of the hype about how quickly the space was growing, it was interested in learning what types of people were actually looking for such degrees. Importantly, it also wanted to know whether its potential customers would be willing to pay a price that would make the entire model viable. Our research uncovered a number of functional and emotional jobs around learning new skills, impressing potential employers, and making family members proud. Although gaining insights into key jobs was helpful, it was insufficient for understanding who would enroll at a traditional four-year college, who would apply for a degree from a technical school, who would seek out an online degree, and who would give up on pursuing higher education entirely. For that, job drivers were essential. By probing deeply into attitudes (e.g., parental and spousal expectations), background (e.g., financial constraints, children), and circumstances (e.g., work schedule, degree-based promotion potential), we were able to identify clear segments that would be interested in an online degree at a price that made sense for both the student and the education company. The company then was able to design a flexible online course structure that made higher education accessible to a customer segment that previously would have given up on their educational pursuits. Using other insights from the Jobs Atlas we created, the company also chose to focus on a few key fields in which there was higher demand and in which it could differentiate itself. As the online space has grown more crowded, this company continues to be recognized as a leader in the areas in which it plays.

Marketers will often talk about demographics and attitudes, and some will talk about functional needs, yet the categories typically get mixed together haphazardly without establishing clear causal mechanisms leading from job drivers to jobs to specific customer purchase and usage behaviors (the subject of the next chapter). A lot gets lost in such messy thinking.

CHAPTER SUMMARY

The road to understanding starts with job drivers, yet it is critical to begin the journey in jobs. If we begin by looking at attitudes, background, and circumstances, we will quickly get lost in details. What we care about are the drivers that lead to key jobs to be done. If a woman buying a car happens to be a vegan, it generally doesn't matter. Once we start the journey with jobs, we can work backward to job drivers. Now we are ready to drive forward to the current approaches used by customers to get those jobs done today and to put the pain points associated with those current approaches into their appropriate context.

Unlike jobs, which are the tasks that customers are looking to get done in their lives, job drivers are not objectives. Job drivers are the underlying contextual elements that make certain jobs more or less important for specific customers.

Customers behave and make decisions differently based on their job drivers, which come in three forms. Customers' attitudes (social or personality-based traits), background (long-term context), and circumstances (immediate or near-term factors) all cause them to prioritize their jobs differently.

Jobs and job drivers combine to yield meaningful customer segments that are based on insight into the "why," not just the "who" or "what." Organizations can target these segments with offerings that register deeply, not ones that simply correlate to underlying demographic characteristics.

3

CURRENT APPROACHES AND PAIN POINTS

HOW CUSTOMERS LOOK AT TODAY'S SOLUTIONS

WE ONCE CAME ACROSS an individual who had made an interesting alteration to his alarm clock. He had added a drop of glue to the top of one of the buttons, creating a slight bump. The problem, as he explained, was that all of the buttons felt more or less the same. This was particularly true as he was reaching blindly above his head in the early hours of the morning after being jarred out of his sleep by the sudden onset of loud music. To make matters worse, 14 of the 15 buttons on the alarm clock would not turn off the alarm. One of those 15 buttons would temporarily quiet the alarm, but that would simply cause the fiendish clock to yet again rouse his sleeping wife 9 minutes later, by which point he had already left for the

GLUE
7:05

shower. This created an entirely different set of problems. Adding glue to the elusive button was this individual's way of alleviating this unwanted morning frustration.

While the glue on the alarm clock may have slightly marred an otherwise stylish appliance, this workaround was far preferable to the pain point that was otherwise annoying both the clock purchaser and another important stakeholder. If only the clock maker had possessed that insight! Understanding what customers do today and how they respond to various pain points broadens the solution space for both incremental and breakthrough innovations.

IN THIS CHAPTER, YOU WILL LEARN:

- How to identify key stakeholders beyond the product purchaser.
- When to replace and when to complement existing customer behaviors.
- How to add value by identifying and solving customer pain points.

LOOKING BEYOND WHO BUYS THE PRODUCT

In many markets, such as with B2B purchases or the public sector, the buyer is not the only person who needs to be satisfied. Buyers' decisions always reflect a careful juggling of the different priorities of multiple stakeholders who will be affected by the decision. It's not enough, therefore, to blackbox a buyer into a single entity. A thorough understanding of how decisions are made requires an identification of key stakeholders, what they are doing, and what bothers them about the process.

Let's look at the grocery industry. A few years back we conducted Jobs research for a client who wanted further insight into people's decision making about what they took home from the store and why. Through the research, we noted that at least three stakeholder types would have distinct requirements in the shelf-to-table flow: the person buying the product, the person preparing the food, and the person eating the food. Certainly, there was often overlap. The person buying the food might also be the one to cook it, for instance, and/or the ultimate diner. But this varied from scenario to scenario. If we had observed only the in-store shopper, we might have assumed that price and fit into established shopping patterns were the most important jobs to satisfy. Had we focused our efforts on the meal preparer, we might have determined that ease of preparation reigned supreme. Had we simply talked to someone who just finished a meal, the level of spiciness might have been the top-of-mind insight. Looking too narrowly would have led to a new product that failed to satisfy important stakeholders.

The easiest way to make sure you are not missing key stakeholders is to create a process map from the customer's perspective (see Figure 3-1). Throughout your research, make sure you are asking about and/or observing each step of the process and noting the specific approaches taken by the customer, starting from the time the customer begins thinking about a job to when that job is satisfied. This step-by-step approach enables you to identify key stakeholders and understand how they influence the way the customer ultimately defines her jobs.

In building out a process map, being as specific as possible will help you identify pain points. A pain point is an area where a customer experiences frustration, boredom, or inefficiency. Pain points are often fertile ground for innovation and therefore merit special attention. Additionally, process maps must also be created for particular occasions, not the average scenario. Thinking back to the grocery scenario, trying to create a process map for the broad category of "shopping for meals" would be too ambiguous. After all, a

SAMPLE PROCESS MAP

Example – Dinner Preparation

Step	Planning	Shopping	Cooking	Eating	Clean-up
Stakeholders Involved	• Mary • Dylan	• Mary • Dylan	• Mary • Rachael (daughter)	• Mary • Dylan • Rachael	• Dylan
Current Approaches	• Mary calls Dylan before leaving work to agree on a protein / type of cuisine	• Alternate who shops • Go up every aisle looking for ideas • Look up recipes on phone	• Rachael does prep while Mary cooks • Talk about day while cooking together	• Eat together at kitchen table • Discuss world events	• Lets pans soak • Loads dishwasher • Cleans pans
Pain Points	• No one remembers what ingredients are in the refrigerator or pantry	• Shopping after work is exhausting • More expensive than shopping with advance planning	• Distractions (e.g., text messages, phone calls) cause delay in preparing meal	• Chicken is dry because of fear of under-cooking	• Feels lonely • Food is stuck on dishes • Pans are hard to get fully clean • Not interesting

Figure 3-1

Tuesday afternoon lunch at work, a Friday night dinner for two, or a Sunday afternoon lunch with the family all result in a unique combination of levers to be pulled. Not only do the functional and emotional jobs vary in each of these situations, but the stakes, challenges, and requirements for success change as well. Designing a compromise-heavy solution that attempts to meet the needs of all these situations is likely to result in a solution that fails to satisfy anyone.

INTEGRATING SOLUTIONS WITH EXISTING BEHAVIOR

Observing current stakeholder behavior affects one of the most crucial decisions you will have to make when designing a new solution—whether to complement current approaches or replace them. If the expectation is that customers will need to alter existing behaviors, it is important to accurately gauge how likely behavior change is and how rapidly it will occur. Consider Kellogg's Breakfast Mates, which launched in the late 1990s and contained cereal, milk, and a spoon all in one package. The company was trying to alleviate pain points associated with rushed mornings while capitalizing on opportunities in the potentially lucrative breakfast-on-the-go market. Unfortunately, the product required customers to make a choice about how to alter their preconceived notions about breakfast. Were they supposed to refrigerate the product and eat chilled cereal? This ran counter to claims that the milk did not need to be refrigerated, and if they were taking the cereal on the go, the milk would warm up anyway. Did this mean that they were supposed to pour warm milk on their cereal? That also did not seem appealing. In the end, customers opted to take neither approach, and the product was soon pulled from the shelves.[1]

Current behaviors may seem dysfunctional, but they represent a powerful tide to swim against. Companies often find that even though they've identified pain points they can resolve, those pain points aren't "painful" enough to motivate a change in behavior. Or consumers are so used to shopping on autopilot that they don't even notice the pain points that the company has deemed important. Those working in the field of international development bump up against the stickiness of established behaviors all the time. Any fieldworker can tell you that getting people to switch the way they do things—even if it radically improves their lives—can be an uphill battle.

Promoting girls' education in post-Taliban Afghanistan is a prime illustration of the difficulties of swimming against the norm.

Afghanistan is widely associated with the Taliban and their draconian policies toward women—burkas, child brides, and no schools for girls. The invasion of Afghanistan by the United States in 2001 and its subsequent nation-building program was geared toward changing some of the more unpalatable practices toward women. The new Afghan government, supported by the United States and other international donors, made girls' education a priority. Under the Taliban, the enrollment of girls in primary school fell from an already low 32 percent to a paltry 6 percent The goal was to get this number up.

The challenge was not in the large cities, such as Kabul, but in rural areas where attitudes toward girls' education remained extremely conservative. In these areas, early attempts to rebuild classrooms, hire female teachers, and boost enrollment failed miserably. Foreign NGOs and the military poured millions of dollars into girls' education and built an untold number of schools, only to find that the buildings were turned into livestock sheds and the girls remained at home. Why didn't their efforts work?

A major obstacle to uptake was the perception that a girls' education program was "foreign driven." Community elders and leaders were consulted only marginally by the international actors hired to improve the Afghan educational system whose efforts—while well meaning—were largely inconsistent with societal norms. In their attempt to "do good," they did not adequately take into consideration the beliefs, preferences, and attitudes of the people they were looking to help. The result was a roadblock on the route to improvement.

Over time, organizations realized they needed to work harder to include men and boys in their gender initiatives in order to avoid backlash and mitigate concerns that a girls' education program was undermining their authority or status. These groups also invited elders and other leading community members to take responsibility for the initiative, even contributing land and labor toward building the schools on their own. This approach—swimming with the tide of attitudes and behaviors—was much more successful.

IDENTIFYING PAIN POINTS

Although customers may be reluctant to part with certain current approaches, they are consistently looking to alleviate pain points. Pain points are problems that inhibit a customer's ability to get a job done. They are things that customers find inefficient, tedious, boring, or frustrating. Consider some of the pain point pairs in maintaining a lawn (see Figure 3-2).

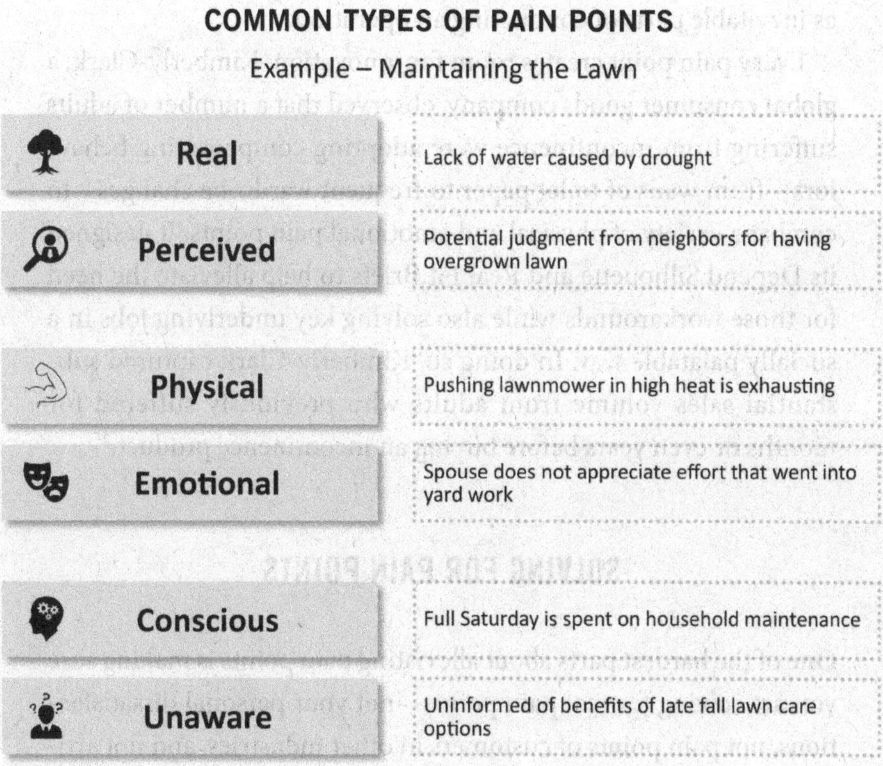
COMMON TYPES OF PAIN POINTS
Example – Maintaining the Lawn
Real
Lack of water caused by drought
Perceived
Potential judgment from neighbors for having overgrown lawn
Physical
Pushing lawnmower in high heat is exhausting
Emotional
Spouse does not appreciate effort that went into yard work
Conscious
Full Saturday is spent on household maintenance
Unaware
Uninformed of benefits of late fall lawn care options

Figure 3-2

While some pain points are obvious and can be quickly captured through common sense or conversations with customers, others are less apparent and are better captured through journal recordings and observations (e.g., process complexity, points of confusion or indecision, accepted workarounds). This phenomenon occurs even in the most rational-seeming environments. For example, a medical technology company we worked with interviewed dozens of surgeons to understand what was challenging about particular surgical procedures. It then hooked up heart rate monitors to those surgeons during the procedure, and the data told a very different story. Surgeons got frustrated when doing repetitive tasks, when they couldn't do their job due to having an obstructed view of the surgical site, and in many other situations that they often took for granted as inevitable parts of conducting an operation.

Every pain point creates room for innovation. Kimberly-Clark, a global consumer goods company, observed that a number of adults suffering from incontinence were adopting compensating behaviors—from wads of toilet paper to frequent wardrobe changes—to combat a variety of physical and emotional pain points. It designed its Depend Silhouette and Real Fit Briefs to help alleviate the need for those workarounds while also solving key underlying jobs in a socially palatable way. In doing so, Kimberly-Clark captured substantial sales volume from adults who previously suffered for months or even years before buying an incontinence product.[2]

SOLVING FOR PAIN POINTS

One of the hardest parts about alleviating pain points is making sure you are solving for real pain points—not your personal dissatisfactions, not pain points of customers in other industries, and not artificial pain points that just happen to be the counterpoints to your product's newest features. One way to help do this is to quantitatively assess the validity of your identified pain points in a large sample. Even though real customers may have pointed out several pain points, it does not necessarily mean that the larger population shares those same issues. Using a quantitative survey, you can map pain points to particular customer segments, ultimately ensuring that you are solving pain points for customers you actually wish to target.

You can also use such surveys to identify priorities among pain points, potentially through a technique such as conjoint analysis. This approach calls for having customers weigh trade-offs. Would you prefer a laptop that has two hours more battery life or that weighs half a pound less? Would you prefer that its keyboard be more resonant or that it be five millimeters thinner? Making trade-offs concrete helps to get at customers' true preferences—the ones you will ultimately see reflected in their buying behavior.

THIS CHAPTER IN PRACTICE— ADDRESSING PAIN POINTS WITH THE CUSTOMER IN MIND

A few years back, we worked with a company that happened to be shifting to a new file management system. Objectively, the new system was a million times better than the system being replaced. It offered increased storage capacity, improved search functions, easier file sharing, and a host of other new features. But in bringing in these new benefits, it eliminated the folder-based system that the company's employees were used to. In fairness, the folder system made certain recurring tasks easier for the employees. And, at the end of the day, the company's employees simply had more faith that they would be able to find what they were looking for in folders—even if it took some digging—than if the information was somehow sorted by these intangible meta tags that had been described to them. As the transition progressed, some employees moved to the new system, others continued using the old system, and a small subset created folder-based workarounds in the new system. Anyone looking for a file needed to run multiple searches that looked through both systems. As you might imagine, the resulting mess was very costly and time-consuming. One of the company's senior executives created a weekly meeting called Sharepoint: The Surge—named after a strategy from the war in Iraq—to resolve all of the complications that were arising. Those who were designing the new system could have developed an alternative that kept the familiar folder-based storage mechanisms. Instead, they doubled down on trying to convince the employees that the approach they knew and loved was inferior. That team learned the hard way that having an objectively better product is meaningless if it cannot solve pain points in a way that aligns with popular current approaches.

CHAPTER SUMMARY

Making a "better" product is the easy part of innovation. The hard part is ensuring that your new product is better for the right people in the right ways. New solutions need to account for the needs of multiple stakeholders, each of whom may have different expectations. At the same time, new offerings need to solve pain points in a way that fits with ingrained behaviors. Understand what's wrong with the status quo, but be wary of engaging in a headlong battle against habit.

The product purchaser may be just one of several stakeholders who will need to be satisfied by your offering. Consider whether other end users or key decision makers will need to be satisfied along the way.

Making a process map—a graphical depiction of each step of the customer's journey from deciding to buy a product to disposing of it—can help identify additional stakeholders, and it can be a good way to spot pain points that are making customers unhappy.

Customers may be willing to change some behaviors to use your product, but not always. Make sure you understand which current approaches will be leveraged and which will be replaced. If you expect customers to change their behavior, remember that such change often occurs slowly.

Customers are routinely looking for new solutions that help them alleviate pain points—the issues that get in the way of satisfying a job to be done. Look beyond those pain points that are obvious to also consider those that are emotional or about which customers are unaware.

Consider trade-offs. It may not be feasible to solve for all pain points at once, so force customers to state priorities through suggesting clear choices.

CHART THE DESTINATION AND ROADBLOCKS

Identify the

SUCCESS CRITERIA

stakeholders will use to determine their interest in a new solution

Investigate the

OBSTACLES

stakeholders will need to overcome for buying or using a new solution

4

SUCCESS CRITERIA

THE CUSTOMER'S DEFINITION OF A WIN

ONCE WE UNDERSTAND THE jobs, job drivers, current approaches, and pain points, can we build a product? Oftentimes, no! Stephen discovered this a decade ago, when a large cell phone company read some of the earliest writings about Jobs to be Done and asked that the framework be used to design a next-generation offering. What did jobs tell us about how to make trade-offs between size and durability, battery life and screen resolution, and a large number of other key design decisions? Too little. The company needed to understand how exactly customers defined the successful accomplishment of priority jobs, in the appropriate contexts (drivers), so that the product would be considered by corporate buyers who were currently using workarounds such as walkie-talkies to enable their workforce to communicate (current approaches and pain points). Key questions had to be answered: How quickly must the device be mastered by new employees? In what specific ways must it excel in looking up a product or a conversation thread about a specific task? It was only by digging into the success criteria that he learned the critical facts necessary to shape the product in these detailed yet essential ways. Success metrics can be numerous, highly specific, and concrete—they are invaluable in telling innovators how to make their ideas into hits.

IN THIS CHAPTER, YOU WILL LEARN:

- How to define success from the customer's perspective rather than management's.
- Where to find opportunities to add value and how to measure your results.
- Why making sacrifices and trade-offs can actually add value to a new solution.

DEFINING SUCCESS

Too little time is spent thinking about how customers will decide whether a new product or service is a success. It's often assumed that the customer will like the new offering, so the conversation focuses on business-oriented metrics—things such as first-year sales figures, breakeven time, and market share captured. Part of the reason we focus on business metrics is that they're more easily measured. No one has come up with a formula or magic number for predicting *ex ante* whether a new product will succeed. Although it would be nice to suggest that you simply need to satisfy two jobs and alleviate three pain points, success is rarely this academic.

At the same time, we've found that the companies that have the greatest success are those that have figured out how to satisfy the *right* jobs and alleviate the *right* pain points. This means honing in on contexts that are particularly important or distressing. It requires understanding what truly motivates your target customer.

The innovation team at Big Heart Pet Brands spent a lot of time with cat owners trying to understand their routines and the relationships they had with their pets.[1] Perhaps unsurprisingly, these relationships are driven by a complex web of emotional jobs punctuated by a number of functional pain points. The Big Heart team found that cat owners are continuously striving to get their independent cats to express affection, with feeding time playing an extremely important role. Dry cat foods are less expensive, less messy, and faster to serve. They can be left out all day, and it is easier to buy them in bulk quantities. At the same time, many cat owners will tell you that their cats prefer the taste, texture, and variety that come with wet foods. Based on the structure of the existing market, pet owners were forced to make a trade-off decision. They needed to choose whether it was more important to satisfy the emotional jobs related to pleasing their cats' tastes or to avoid the functional pain points associated with wet foods. So with this constraint standing in the way, how did Big Heart meet the customer's definition of success? It challenged the existing product category structure (which is driven primarily by supply chain issues) and avoided the wet/dry dichotomy altogether.

Big Heart took its insights into the jobs and pain points of its customers and developed a new product concept—a cat food with a dry exterior but a wet, meaty center. It tested exceptionally well with customers. Through rapid prototyping and continuous product improvement, Big Heart was ultimately able to create a product that consumers would love and that the company could cost-effectively manufacture at scale. The new product line—Meow Mix Tender Centers—won on both the functional and emotional levels, alleviating the need for the customer to choose between the two. As a result, combined sales for the first two years exceeded $100 million, a feat that has been achieved with only three pet food launches in the past five years. By focusing on an important aspect of the pet relationship—one charged with emotional concerns—the Big Heart team was able to satisfy customers in a big way.

MEASURING SUCCESS

Figuring out how to win in established markets can be difficult enough. As innovative companies begin to compete asymmetrically—by winning along previously unconsidered dimensions of performance—the very definition of a win can change, making the task that much harder. Let's look closely at the Tesla Model S, named the Best Overall car for 2014 and 2015 by Consumer Reports.[2] Consumer Reports chooses its top car picks based on three criteria: performance, reliability, and safety. Performance is further broken down into traditional characteristics around handling, capacity, and comfort, while reliability and safety are based on user-reported problems and crash test results, respectively. In some ways, traditional success criteria can be cross-applied for the Model S. Safety ratings, for example, are still an important measure of success. However, when the P85D version of the Model S broke the Consumer Reports rating system—scoring 103 points out of a possible 100—it became clear that traditional success criteria are insufficient for judging the Model S.[3]

To understand how Tesla is redefining the very notion of a perfect car, we need to think about what the Model S actually is, using Jobs language. The Model S is an electric vehicle, which makes it much more than simply a transportation choice. The new technology expands the range of jobs that people can satisfy to include a number that are not transportation related. Driving an electric car, for example, not only gets you where you want to go but also allows you to act on environmental concerns. The addition of this new dimension, however, means that the car will be assessed across a range of standards—some familiar (safety, comfort, reliability) and some completely new (refueling/recharging times, ability to travel long distances). The Model S wins because it does an exceptionally good job satisfying both the traditional and newly relevant jobs that customers buying an electric car want to satisfy.

COMMON STRATEGIES FOR CREATING SUCCESS

	Strategy	Example
Less	Reduce the effort, time, resources, or money customers must expend to satisfy a job	Simple Bank – Online bank that eliminates common fees and reduces the effort needed to budget for expenses
Less	Eliminate the confusion or complexity of using the product	iPhone – Phone that has fewer capabilities than its Android counterparts, but vastly simplifies the user experience
More	Increase the number of jobs a customer can satisfy	Microsoft Office – Suite of computer programs that allows users to address a broad range of business challenges across job titles
More	Improve the quality of the end product or the speed of carrying out the task	Swiffer – A sweeping tool that makes it extremely quick to remove light debris from floors
More	Enhance the ease or comfort of using the product	OXO – Kitchen products that add a premium feel to basic tools (e.g., vegetable peelers with comfortable grips, no-bend measuring cups)
Balance	Balance the satisfaction of functional and emotional jobs	Vanguard Target Funds – Self-adjusting mutual funds that help you save for retirement while reducing worries about keeping up with economic changes
Balance	Allow satisfaction among a wider variety of users or stakeholders	Kix – Breakfast cereal that tastes good for children, but meets nutritional standards of parents ("Kid tested, mother approved")

Figure 4-1

Beyond just satisfying jobs, however, it's important to understand *how* customers want to satisfy those jobs. More is not always better. Satisfying customers' jobs means knowing what they want more of, what they want less of, and where they are looking to strike a balance. To help get you started, we put together a list of common strategies for tying success criteria back to key Jobs principles (see Figure 4-1).

By understanding the details of what customers demand, companies can use that knowledge to compete asymmetrically. They can change the perception of what an industry is supposed to deliver and leverage overlooked assets that give them an advantage over established or stronger competitors.

Let's look at how a bold upstart is challenging an industry behemoth in this way. For years, Microsoft Outlook has been the king of business email. And for what seems like just as long, young tech companies have come to the table announcing how they have the next big application that will finally be the death of email. Yet email thrives.

While attempts at email replacement have come and gone, Slack has come to the table with something different. Instead of trying to replace email—which isn't what customers are asking for—Slack has focused on identifying what customers want more of and what they want less of, ultimately creating an offering that strikes a balance. Slack is one of the fastest-growing new business applications. It's an office messaging app that works with email rather than trying to replace it outright.

Slack focuses on making internal communication easier. It offers a fast, informal way to talk to coworkers, but it retains the archiving abilities of traditional email, even improving on the ability to search old messages. Email continues to be used, especially for external communications, but Slack helps reduce the volume of messages in your inbox, while simultaneously reducing the need for time-consuming face-to-face meetings. In part, this is because the app lets users search and access shared files on their own, without having to question other team members. When questions are necessary, workers can provide quick answers and status updates in a side window, reducing clutter in their inboxes. As the number of Slack users has grown to over a million, teams using the app have praised its ability to improve efficiency. By understanding where to cut and where to add, Slack has reached a $3.8 billion valuation in just over two years.[4]

It is critical to understand that some seemingly minor variables can actually be quite important because they are used as ways to measure whether certain jobs are getting done. For Brookwood, the independent school mentioned earlier in this book, parents' success criteria include the breadth of course offerings (showing that the school attends to the varied interests of its students), student body diversity (ensuring that children emerge from their education well grounded), and parental access to the educational program (illustrating the school's commitment to forging a partnership in a child's schooling).

CREATING VALUE THROUGH TRADE-OFFS

A customer-centric lens allows companies to understand how they can make trade-offs to increase value. Deeply understanding customer demand allows you to shift from spending on unnecessary, overvalued attributes and invest in important jobs that the market underappreciates and that will make a difference. In 1996, MSNBC launched into the small but developing cable news space. After years of finishing third in the three-company race—competing against CNN and Fox News—MSNBC adopted a new model in time for the 2008 U.S. presidential election. The new model reduced spending on overpriced TV talent that fit a certain image, realizing that cable news viewers were more interested in what hosts had to say than in what they looked like. MSNBC could spend less money by hiring talent with stronger backgrounds in political science, such as former radio personalities and print media journalists, but with less on-air TV experience. At the same time, MSNBC delivered more of what its target audience sought: political commentary. This meant that MSNBC could place less emphasis on gathering and verifying facts, an expensive process that is better handled by other established news sources. According to the Pew Research Center, MSNBC's content is 85 percent opinion, while Fox News delivers 55 percent opinion and CNN delivers 46 percent opinion.[5] Even though the 2008 election was a polarizing time, likely causing a surge in MSNBC's popularity among viewers seeking a liberal forum, the model has continued to prove successful for MSNBC. By 2012, MSNBC had the lowest production costs per viewer but finished second in average primetime viewership (see Figure 4-2). From 2011 to 2012, MSNBC also saw a 20 percent increase in viewership among the highly sought after 25- to 54-year-old demographic, while Fox News saw a 1 percent increase.[6]

What these examples illustrate is that customers value products that succeed in the areas that matter most to them. At the same time,

PRODUCTION COSTS FOR MAJOR CABLE NEWS NETWORKS

	Fox News	CNN	MSNBC
Cost of news production (2012)	$820,000,000	$682,000,000	$240,000,000
Primetime average viewership (2012)	2,071,000	670,000	913,000
Production cost per viewer	$396	$1,018	$283

Figure 4-2

managing production costs and product complexity may require lowering performance in areas that matter less. The issue that remains, then, is how to find areas to deprioritize without upsetting your customers. After all, don't we all feel a little irked when the airline cuts leg room by another inch or our favorite snack disappears from shelves in a product line simplification effort? (What ever happened to Tostitos Gold? They were thick enough that they never broke even in the heartiest of dips!) This brings us back to the importance of job drivers and customer segmentation. Although it may not be possible to please everyone, understanding how customers cluster together lets you determine the contexts in which your products will be used, as well as how prevalent those contexts are in the general population.

Consider the achievement of the Colgate Wisp, one of the boldest innovations in the multicentury history of the toothbrush. By most standards, the Wisp—a flimsy, small, single-use brush with a tiny minted pearl in the center of its miniscule bristles—isn't a great device. It cleans a modicum of plaque, no tartar, and little in the cracks and crevices where mouth nasties get started. It's not electric and features no cartoon characters. However, it narrowly targets a precise job: cleaning your mouth when you're outside your home. Users measure success by criteria including removal of obvious pieces of food, freshening the taste of their mouths, speediness of use, and not having to spit (an etiquette no-no in shared workplace bathrooms). By delivering on these criteria and little else, the Wisp has become a big brand and created a totally new source of growth for Colgate.

THIS CHAPTER IN PRACTICE—DETERMINING WHERE TO EXCEL

When Stephen rolled out Africa's first mobile commerce platform in 2002 (for the Celtel phone network that is now owned by India's

Airtel), the first customers were large businesses like South African Breweries (SAB) that sought to streamline the payment process for big deliveries. SAB's finance staff wanted clear proof that the new solution would help them accomplish two jobs: speed deliveries and reduce fraud. Establishing the success criteria for each job helped Celtel design the detailed parameters of the system. For instance, the system should reduce the number of times money was counted from seven to no more than two. It should save an hour per night from the reconciliation process once drivers returned with their empty trucks. It should essentially eliminate the problem of delivery truck driver-instigated fraud. Having these clear parameters in place enabled Celtel to know where to invest, such as in educating distributors receiving the beer as well as finance staff at the depot, and what could be left for later, such as creating a beautiful interface. Knowing the key jobs was vital but not enough. Success criteria enabled the design of an appropriate solution—and nothing beyond what was actually needed.

CHAPTER SUMMARY

Success criteria translate jobs into highly actionable parameters. They must be tied to jobs, and they may be important only because they are used as proxies for whether certain jobs are being addressed. Criteria are often impacted by customers' attitudes, background, and circumstances. Sometimes they are tangibly measurable, although just because some are not—emotions, for example—doesn't mean they don't count. Fulfilling the success criteria gives customers a reason to believe that you will accomplish their overarching jobs. Because success criteria are typically numerous, they provide innovators with detailed guidance on how customers determine that a job has gotten done, in what context, and how a new solution will be assessed as beating its alternatives. They provide a critical step between customer insight and determining product features. In this way, they enable ideas to become well-articulated concepts.

Success criteria can be captured by focusing on occasions and contexts that are most important to the customer.

You can measure success by evaluating how well your product can satisfy key customer jobs. Understand what customers want more of, what they want less of, and where they seek balance. Determine how they will measure success, using proxies and other approaches that make sense through their eyes.

The definition of a win may change as other companies compete asymmetrically and alter customer expectations for what an industry or product category will deliver.

Additional value can be created by making trade-offs. It's perfectly acceptable to give up on certain features that matter to only a limited number of customers. Focus on excelling along the dimensions that matter to your target customer segments.

5

OBSTACLES

WHAT HOLDS NEW IDEAS BACK

WHILE RESEARCHING THE FOOD and beverage sector a few years back, we came across a young woman living in what she described as a "unique" apartment. It had no kitchen. We don't mean that the apartment had a small kitchen, or that the kitchen wasn't separated with walls. We mean that there was no kitchen. No oven. No burners. No kitchen sink. You get the idea. When we talked to her about the idea of moving, she acknowledged that she had planned to find a new place, but after a while she didn't really mind the quirks so much. Plus moving is such a hassle. Other things came up, and the idea of moving became much less of a priority.

The spread of new products works in a similar way. There may be some early adopters who are excited about the new offering, but many people will sit back and wait until their circumstances dictate a change. Beyond general inertia, specific obstacles to adoption and use can also depress new product sales. Had our client released an oven-prepared meal, our kitchenless friend wouldn't have purchased it. While the lack of a kitchen may be a somewhat atypical hurdle, we'll use this chapter to look at some of the more common factors that stop customers from buying or using enticing new products.

IN THIS CHAPTER, YOU WILL LEARN:

- How inertia impacts even the greatest innovations.
- What slows the adoption of new products.
- What gets in the way of customers using and repurchasing new products.

THE FIGHT AGAINST INERTIA

Just because there is a better product or a better way of doing something, it doesn't mean that customers will embrace the new solution. If a new offering doesn't fit with engrained behaviors and expectations, customers will be reluctant to change and will look for reasons not to shift to a new solution. Companies will be forced to invest resources fighting both actual and perceived obstacles.

In many parts of the world, mopeds are a popular way of navigating congested urban areas. Despite similar traffic and hassles in many U.S. cities, mopeds have never really taken off in the States. Part of that can be attributed to perception. When you think about mopeds in other parts of the world, you often think of old, loud, dirty contraptions that—while practical—aren't particularly comfortable or esteemed. We think of them being used to carry families of four down dusty roads in South America or through crowded traffic jams in India. Back in America, we just don't see the need. If we want to get around the city, public transportation is typically good enough to get the job done. When it's not, cars are becoming more and more luxurious. Cars give us the option to turn on our seat warmers, sip our coffee, make a phone call or two, and belt out the lyrics to the newest Taylor Swift song completely free of judgment. You can't do that on a moped. And with favorable lease terms, a car can actually be pretty affordable.

But things are changing, and cars aren't always ideal. Parking costs are starting to soar. Gas is getting more expensive, and people are becoming more environmentally conscious. Cities—though historically designed around cars in the United States—are making strides to be friendlier for bikes and mopeds. People are getting married later, delaying the move out of urban areas. Even families are choosing cities over suburbs with increasing frequency. As urban areas become even more densely populated, cars begin to make less sense. And when you need to carry groceries or bulky items home from the store, public transportation is less than ideal. There's clearly a market opening for mopeds in U.S. cities, but consumers are going to need to be convinced. They're not going to shoulder the burden of determining why mopeds are actually a good idea. Companies need to be well aware of stubborn behaviors that can impede the successful uptake of their new product and think, from the very outset of the design process, how they can excite people out of their comfort zone.

GenZe has taken a number of steps to fight inertia and nonconsumption, in hopes that its new electric scooter will take off among younger, urban consumers in the United States. Before launching its new bike (the GenZe 2.0), company employees traveled to cities around the country to talk to people about how they were commuting today, where they were experiencing pain points, and what they were trying to get done in their commutes. Using that knowledge, they designed a bike that accounts for the jobs and job drivers of their target demographic. It offers cargo units to carry briefcases, groceries, and other personal items. Those units are even rainproof for people in cities with less forgiving climates. The scooters are environmentally friendly, allowing riders to save on fuel costs and feel as though they're

FIVE WAYS TO FIGHT INERTIA

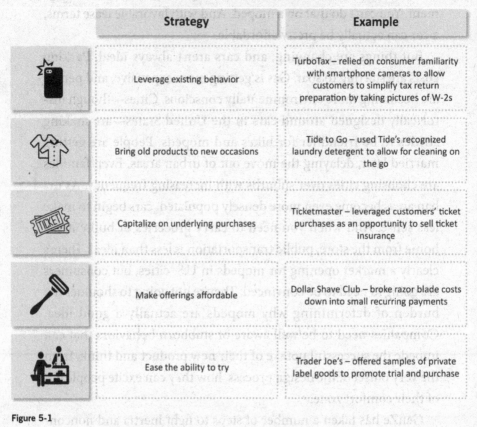

	Strategy	Example
	Leverage existing behavior	TurboTax – relied on consumer familiarity with smartphone cameras to allow customers to simplify tax return preparation by taking pictures of W-2s
	Bring old products to new occasions	Tide to Go – used Tide's recognized laundry detergent to allow for cleaning on the go
	Capitalize on underlying purchases	Ticketmaster – leveraged customers' ticket purchases as an opportunity to sell ticket insurance
	Make offerings affordable	Dollar Shave Club – broke razor blade costs down into small recurring payments
	Ease the ability to try	Trader Joe's – offered samples of private label goods to promote trial and purchase

Figure 5-1

doing their part for the environment. The scooters are also visually appealing and tech-heavy, featuring a 7-inch touch-screen control panel. Consumers don't choose the GenZe 2.0 because they can't afford something better; they choose it to make a statement. The bike also helps lower the barriers to adoption by introducing features that make it safer and easier to use, such as taller windscreens and a special driving mode for those still learning to ride. While it remains to be seen how well the GenZe 2.0 will do in the United States, GenZe's dedication to customer centricity and its focus on defeating traditional purchase obstacles will give it the best possible chance to succeed.

Fighting inertia means lowering the barriers to trying a new product. While some companies continually "wow" their loyal customers with a parade of shiny new products, most do not. This latter group has to work hard to induce trial. We created a chart that illustrates several ways companies have found success in improving the speed of product diffusion (see Figure 5-1).

While these strategies can help fight inertia, other obstacles may also stand in the way of customers adopting or using your new product. The next two sections identify ten of the most common obstacles that slow the spread of your new product.

OBSTACLES TO ADOPTION

Obstacles to adoption are barriers that prevent customers from buying your products in the first place. Even customers who might benefit from your product—or otherwise be inclined to buy it—may choose a competitor's product or nonconsumption in the face of these obstacles. Therefore, it is important to find ways to reduce or eliminate them. The following obstacles are some of the most frequent barriers to product purchases:

Lack of knowledge. One of the most fundamental reasons that customers don't buy your product is that they don't know they need it. It's not that the innovator is making up a job to be done that didn't actually exist—a tough road to take, for sure—but rather that customers had just gotten used to the old way of doing things. Look at medical records at a physician's office, which are typically a mess of free-form text, checked boxes, and scans of faxes from diagnostic labs and other doctors. It's very tough to find useful information quickly, and sometimes critical data gets overlooked. Yet vendors of "golden record" solutions that create a single integrated file have found the market slow to materialize because physicians don't realize the cost—in terms of both money and suboptimal medical outcomes—of the current make-do approach. Only by quantifying the situation and evangelizing about the dangers of the typical practice have they made people realize that these jobs can get done in a far better way.

Behavior change requirement. As we saw when we looked at current approaches and pain points, getting people to change their behavior can be difficult. Ozon, often referred to as the Amazon of Russia, is the largest e-commerce company in Russia. It started with book sales, moved into movies and music, ventured into consumer electronics, then ultimately became a full-range retailer of virtually every consumer good imaginable. Despite its relative size in Russia, growth has been challenging in Russia's cash-based economy. In particular, Ozon has had trouble selling its proprietary e-reader (the Ozon Galaxy), e-books, and digital music. With digital content requiring a credit card for purchase and Russian consumers being generally unwilling or unable to move away from cash, these categories have seen lackluster sales.[1]

Multiple decision makers. Even great ideas can be hindered by the need to bring many disconnected decision makers on board, some of whom may have misaligned incentives. Systems that enable teams of doctors to consult online about shared cases seem to make a ton of sense, but they have grown quite slowly. IT, hospital departments, and individual physicians all need to come on board, or else the system will be stymied. Some of these entities may embrace change, whereas others see mainly risk. Even if the benefits of the solution are clear to all, simply getting people to agree on a proposition and action plan can take far longer than implementing the actual system.

High costs. Costs can be high in a number of ways. The actual cost of a new product can be prohibitively expensive. At around $40,000 (or roughly 80 percent of the median U.S. household income), a Nesmuk diamond-studded knife is simply too expensive for most consumers. A product can also be too costly compared to rival goods. Harrods, the UK department store, launched its £29.95 Pot Noodle in 2008. Although the launch was part of a stunt to celebrate design innovation (while also sending proceeds to charity), one can't help but wonder whether that price is a bit high for a cup of instant noodles.[2] Finally, the cost of switching to a new solution can be unpalatable. Along this third vein, cell phone carriers decided years ago that they would make it hard to switch carriers by imposing an early termination fee. More recently, as carriers have battled for market share, they have begun buying out termination fees from other carriers and eliminating the idea of a standard two-year contract altogether, thus helping to reduce the costs of switching carriers.

High risk. Customers will be reluctant to adopt a new solution if it involves a lot of risk or a high potential cost of failure. Even with the recent rise in lawsuits by patent trolls, the uptake of patent litigation insurance has been slow. In part, attorneys believe that this is because buying such insurance might actually invite patent suits with liabilities that quickly exceed coverage limits.[3] Even though the insurance could prevent crippling lawsuit damages, the risk of attracting patent troll attention has been too great to allow for fast adoption.

Unfamiliar category. Sometimes, products are so innovative that they define a new category that the customer doesn't really understand or have a budget for. Consider the Internet of Things (IoT)—a network of potentially millions of connected devices and sensors in a workplace that can keep tabs on just about everything happening in a facility. For all of the hype surrounding the idea, uptake by major corporations has been slow. There typically isn't anyone with IoT in the job title or with an IoT line item in the annual budget. IoT vendor en-Gauge has addressed this challenge in a clever way, focusing tightly on monitoring the readiness of fire extinguishers. Fire safety usually is someone's responsibility, and few people dissent from spending modestly to improve a company's readiness in this area. Once en-Gauge introduces its IoT solution through this route, it plans to be in prime position to sell much more expansive offerings later.[4]

OBSTACLES TO USE

A second set of obstacles to consider are **obstacles to use**. These are the reasons that customers stop using your product or service after initial adoption. Obstacles to use can take a few different shapes. You may see an early wave of enthusiasm with a rapid falloff of purchases. Or, more straightforwardly, people simply stop repurchasing your product, buying add-on features, or upgrading to later editions. Obstacles to use present a major hurdle to creating a sustainable business model. The following categories represent some of the most common reasons a customer will not use a product:

Limited supporting infrastructure. Sometimes a product can be great on its own, but lacks value without a system to support it. Imagine downloading a peer-to-peer app but having no peers! Similarly, electric vehicles offer a number of benefits for both drivers and the environment. Yet even ecofriendly consumers who are willing to buy electric cars are often dissuaded by the lack of available charging stations. Those who drive long distances arguably have the most to save (assuming the price of gas stays high relative to the price of electricity in your area), but they are the ones for whom the solution is least viable. Without the infrastructure that allows you to get the full potential out of your purchase, use becomes prohibitively difficult.

Use creates pain points. Customers will not continue to use a product that is overly complex or difficult to use. Yet companies often insist on overloading their new products with features rather than focusing on satisfying important jobs well. According to an NPD Group survey of over 1,500 consumers, 13 percent of consumers had returned an electronic device due to frustration when trying to get it to work.[5] Windows Vista, launched by Microsoft in 2007, was surrounded by high expectations from both consumers and the company. As incessant compatibility and performance problems plagued the product, even some of Microsoft's most loyal customers defected for Apple.

It's cool, not better. Many times, a new product sounds really exciting, but it ultimately doesn't do a better job than the existing solution. Generally, customers rush to try these products but stop using these solutions when they realize that they don't excel along the dimensions that they find most important. The technology that allows you to purchase items using a cell phone has been around for a relatively long time. Although a number of people tried it once or twice, they ultimately found that it didn't perform any better than a standard swipe of the credit card. In fact, it often took longer. As Google and Apple reignite the race to get mobile payments off the ground, this second wave is focusing on jobs that are now top of mind for customers, such as data security.

Offering isn't targeted. Similarly, new offerings need to be targeted to specific jobs and customer types. The Segway was another fun device that was launched without much purpose or direction. Once the company stopped trying to sell the Segway to the general public—who couldn't afford it and didn't know what to do with it—it found success among customer types with undersatisfied jobs, including police forces, urban tour guides, and warehouses.

Getting customers to even consider your product in the first place can often be quite the challenge, but finding ways to overcome obstacles to long-term use can be just as important a task. Without opportunities to resell to past purchasers, you may find that your business model is simply unsustainable.

THIS CHAPTER IN PRACTICE—FIGHTING INERTIA IN E-COMMERCE

When we started a project for a major retailer, the kickoff team identified Amazon as a major competitor. It made sense. The retailer's website had a relatively small share of online consumer spending in its merchandise category, and analyst reports suggested that the retailer's prices were frequently being undercut. Nevertheless, as the company looked to build its e-commerce presence, it became clear that Amazon was actually doing the retailer a favor. As it turns out, Amazon was doing several things to fight consumer inertia and lower the obstacles to online shopping in the category. First, by visibly promoting the sale of the product category online, Amazon raised awareness that the retailer's products could be affordably purchased online despite how heavy they were on average. Second, by allowing consumers to buy the products as an add-on to other Amazon purchases, Amazon helped normalize the idea of routinely shopping online in the category. Third, Amazon's prices forced the retailer to reconsider and optimize its own shipping mechanisms, ultimately reducing its costs and increasing its ability to pass cost savings on to the consumer. While Amazon may ultimately be more of a competitor than a partner, its own actions are currently helping to defeat obstacles to adoption industry-wide. Our client decided to piggyback on the behaviors Amazon was already introducing, using its superior selection and local store pickup option to compete in ways that Amazon could not.

CHAPTER SUMMARY

Getting consumers interested in a new product can be an uphill battle. For the most part, consumers already have a set list of products that they regularly buy or consider for satisfying a particular job. Alternatives need to be compelling enough to shake consumers out of their routines. By lowering the obstacles to buying a new product—such as by making it inexpensive to try or by being clear about its benefits—companies may be able to win over early adopters, who will then act as reference customers that tout your product's benefits to others. To ensure long-term success, companies also need to eliminate the barriers to use, thus ensuring that customers have a reason to turn to your organization again after the first sale has been completed.

People are creatures of habit, and they tend to change their behaviors and buying habits slowly. Simply creating enticing products may not be enough to get people to take a chance on your new offering. The burden will be on the organization—not the customer—

to defeat any excuses that justify maintaining the status quo.

Help build demand for your product by making it easy for people to learn about your product and give it a shot. In particular, six common obstacles inhibit customers from adopting a new solution: lack of knowledge, a required change in behavior, the presence of multiple decision makers, high costs, high risk, and a lack of familiarity with the product category.

Continuously acquiring a new customer base is often too costly to be sustainable. Eliminate obstacles to using your new product so that first-time buyers become repeat buyers. Four obstacles routinely get in the way of customers continuing to use and repurchase your products: limited supporting infrastructure, pain points created by use of the product, an inability to excel over the competition, and poor customer targeting.

MAKE THE TRIP WORTHWHILE

Assess the

VALUE

of the solutions that your organization might offer

Beat the

COMPETITION

by defining the playing field broadly and using your advantages

6

VALUE

HOW INSIGHTS BECOME REVENUE

IN 1989, STEPHEN HAD one of the worst jobs of his life. He was a door-to-door meat salesman. While the job was pretty poor—selling a new type of processed food to food service establishments—the idea was actually a good one. His employer was one of the first companies in the United States to offer *sous vide,* a method through which food is cooked inside a vacuum-sealed plastic bag, sealing in juices and freshness.

The company had not calculated what value this would create for food service customers, so it priced its offerings on a cost-plus basis. The cheapest item on the menu was the least costly to produce—chicken tarragon. It was pretty awful. Unfortunately, when potential customers wanted to try the offerings, this is what they opted for. Disaster. One day, however, a deli owner tried the fish, and he reported back to Stephen that it was fantastic. More importantly, he could never serve fish before because of the smell and freshness issues, but *sous vide* cooking in a pot of boiling water solved these problems. He was the only deli in the area to be able to offer fish, which made him stand out and feel proud. Jobs to be Done! The value created had nothing to do with the price of the ingredients. Understanding the real sources of value enabled the company to position itself in entirely new ways.

IN THIS CHAPTER, YOU WILL LEARN:

- How to calculate how much money is at stake with respect to a new potential solution.
- How to determine how expensive your new solutions can be.
- Whether your proposed business model will support sustained sales of your new solution.

HOW MUCH MONEY IS AT STAKE

When you're trying to pitch a new idea, someone will undoubtedly ask how big the opportunity really is. So how do we know how fast a market will grow or how much of the market will be interested in your solution? With time, concept tests and prototype demonstrations will help refine your estimates. In the early stages, however, the Jobs-based insights you've uncovered can be quite enlightening. By the time you get to market sizing, you'll already know what jobs customers are looking to get done, what pain points they want to eliminate, and what job drivers are pushing them to prioritize some jobs and pain points over others. Quantitative surveys can help you assign hard numbers to the insights in your Jobs Atlas, ultimately giving you the data you need to create a robust customer segmentation that more accurately predicts purchasing behavior. Benchmarks that illustrate how similar jobs have been satisfied in other industries or through other product lines can help further refine market size estimates.

Beyond more accurately measuring market size, Jobs-based thinking allows you to design solutions in a way that actually expands that market potential. In the early 1970s, Mars overtook Hershey as the leading candy company in the United States, and it continued to expand its market share through the end of the decade. By the early 1980s, Hershey realized it needed a new strategy. Through rigorous customer research, Hershey gathered a number of important insights. Perhaps most importantly, Hershey learned that children are not the biggest consumers of candy. In fact, Hershey learned that adults age 18 and older were consuming 55 percent of all candy sold.[1] Hershey used that knowledge to design and market confections that helped adults satisfy latent emotional needs, retaking its position as the U.S. confection leader and expanding the overall candy market. To this day, Hershey continues to innovate based on the jobs to be done of adults. Part of Hershey's focus, for example, has been on helping adults reward or treat themselves in guilt-free ways, such as through its 2011 acquisition of Brookside's relatively healthy fruit-infused dark chocolate.[2] With its focus on products for adults, Hershey continues to lead the U.S. chocolate market.

HOW EXPENSIVE OFFERINGS CAN BE

Part of the calculation of how big a market can grow is a determination of the price at which you will sell your product. In well-established markets, this may not be too much of a consideration. Competitor-based pricing—a strategy that involves copying your competitors' prices or discounting below them to attract market share—will dictate a range of acceptable prices. If most video game makers are selling their games for around $60, you're not likely to have much success selling a game for $120. You might do a calculation to determine whether the optimal price point (based on a combination of volume and price) is $60 or $65, but the range worthy of consideration will be quite small. And in industries like the video game industry—where a relatively small number of game publishers tend to set strict price controls for retailers—there may be limits on how far from the established pricing scheme you can drift.[3]

In less established markets, things begin to change. Some companies try to minimize risk by adopting a basic cost-plus pricing model. They figure out what the solution will cost to make, then mark up the price to create a margin that they know management will be happy with. Ultimately, however, this strategy is somewhat arbitrary, and it may not coincide with the marketing or branding strategy you have laid out for the product. A better alternative—value-based pricing—allows you to set a price based on how well your product can satisfy customers' jobs to be done. Using this strategy, the price you choose can help reframe how customers perceive your product, and it can also focus attention on the emotional jobs your product satisfies.

Let's think again about Uber. At first glance, it may have appeared that Uber was going to adopt a standard competitor-based pricing approach. After all, much of the early conversation about Uber was that it was a cheap alternative to taxis. Depending on the market you're in, however, the service now offers a pretty wide range of price points (including UberPOOL, UberX, UberBLACK, and UberLUX) depending on the jobs you're looking to satisfy. Customers who decide that cost isn't everything can choose to pay more—and in some cases, much more—to ensure a private ride and direct route with no stops, enjoy a more comfortable ride, and impress others by showing up at their destination in style. Adding another layer of complexity, Uber also uses "surge pricing," charging higher prices when demand increases, such as during rush hour or when the weather is bad. While a competitor-based pricing model or a cost-plus model would suggest that prices should remain relatively static even as demand increases, surge pricing makes complete sense under a value-based pricing model. As certain jobs become more important or customers realize new jobs (such as preserving a pair of expensive shoes or arriving on time in unfavorable weather conditions), a value-based pricing strategy suggests that fares should rise as well. While these higher prices may turn some off, they also help cement the idea that Uber isn't just a cheap taxi alternative; it's an on-demand car service that's catering to you.

Although the exact right price may require a detailed pricing analysis, several easy testing methods (such as mock sales, A/B testing, and feature purchasing tests) can help you choose a reasonable starting point for your analysis. Chapter 12 provides a more in-depth look at some of the tools you can use to help gauge customer interest.

TURNING YOUR VALUE PROPOSITION INTO A BUSINESS MODEL

While the Jobs Roadmap is based on the idea of creating value that the customer recognizes and appreciates, this works only if the model also creates value for the business. While finalized business plans need to contain a lot of detail, requiring that much information at the early stages unnecessarily slows down projects. Instead, we have created a five-step litmus test to help you determine whether early ideas will be viable both for attracting new customers and for allowing you to continue to sell to them for the long term (see Figure 6-1). While this assessment is far from comprehensive, it should help you think through some of the deal-breaker risks that might merit taking some ideas off the table.

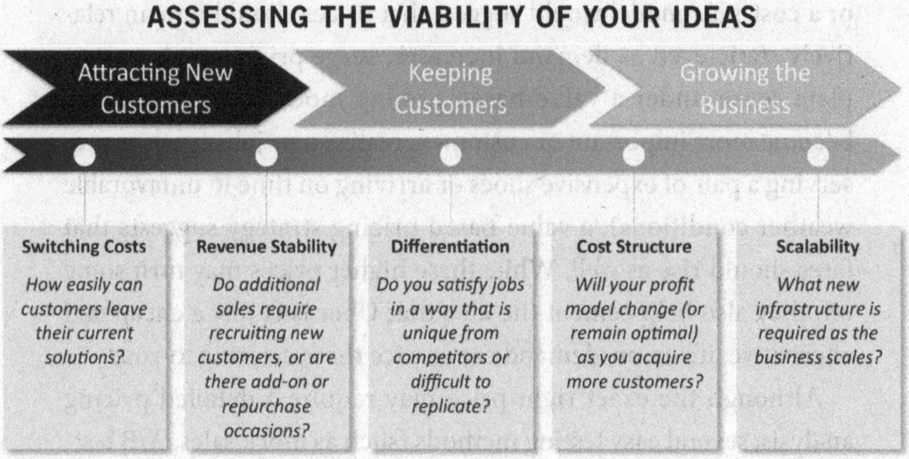
ASSESSING THE VIABILITY OF YOUR IDEAS
Attracting New Customers
Keeping Customers
Growing the Business
Switching Costs
How easily can customers leave their current solutions?
Revenue Stability
Do additional sales require recruiting new customers, or are there add-on or repurchase occasions?
Differentiation
Do you satisfy jobs in a way that is unique from competitors or difficult to replicate?
Cost Structure
Will your profit model change (or remain optimal) as you acquire more customers?
Scalability
What new infrastructure is required as the business scales?

Figure 6-1

Beyond acting as a customer lens for creating new products and services, the Jobs Roadmap is also useful for finding ways to optimize existing processes and business models, or to take costs out of the core business. Boston-based Tasting Counter, which opened in 2015, is a restaurant that has recently started offering a different take on the standard restaurant experience. Instead of making reservations, guests purchase tickets in advance for a meal at a specific time and date in the future. These tickets include the price of the meal, tax, and tip. From a Jobs-based perspective, the restaurant markets itself as satisfying several jobs that ordinary restaurants either don't address or satisfy poorly. Because it exclusively offers a set tasting menu that heavily features local ingredients—many of which are sourced from partner food companies on-site—Tasting Counter ensures that every customer can experience variety and support local businesses. And by having customers pay in advance, it completely removes the financial element from the meal, allowing customers to focus on the food experience without worrying about the price of a particular entrée or the cost of an extra drink. From a business model perspective, those same customer benefits are also benefits to the business. By having a set menu of ingredients and sourcing from local partners, Tasting Counter can reduce its food costs and virtually eliminate waste. It knows exactly how many customers are going to be eating in the restaurant at any given time, allowing the restaurant to order food and bring in staff accordingly. And by having meals paid for in advance, Tasting Counter can actually use and earn interest on money that wouldn't even be in hand with a traditional model. Through focusing on and branding around a few key jobs, Tasting Counter has been able to adopt an incredibly savvy business model.

THIS CHAPTER IN PRACTICE—
CREATING VALUE FOR AN UNDERSERVED SENIOR MARKET

The number of babies being born every year has been on the decline in the developed world. People are also living longer. From an anthropological perspective, this means that populations in developed countries have been aging rapidly. From a business perspective, this means that senior care products represent one of the fastest-growing product categories in high-spending markets. The consumer products company Kimberly-Clark turned to its Global Innovation Center in South Korea to understand what business potential these trends unlocked. As Hari Nair—then the center's global managing director—explained, South Korea's seniors are more likely to remain active than elderly customers in other Asian countries, and South Korea's unique dynamics make the country a good predictor for what other parts of the world will experience years into the future.[4]

When we reached out to Mr. Nair, he explained to us how the innovation team at Kimberly-Clark is using Jobs-based thinking to reframe the senior care market.

> We often think of a platform competing against a similar platform rather than thinking about segmenting the market based on why customers hire our products. At the front end of innovation, we have found that identifying the next big opportunity comes from looking at the jobs that moms, or families, or seniors are trying to satisfy.

Indeed, the team has uncovered a range of functional and emotional jobs, including helping seniors feel secure when traveling alone, helping them stay active, assisting them with leaving a legacy, and helping them stay happy even after their children have left the home.

Based on the insights uncovered by the team's jobs-based research, Kimberly-Clark launched the Golden Friends brand in Korea, which is specifically targeted to help the country's active seniors. The company was able to attract and retain a devoted group of customers who were initially purchasing its disposable undergarments. Playing off this loyalty, the brand's portfolio grew to include other products that interest this group, such as comfortable shoes and walking aids. While we can't go into detail about Kimberly-Clark's plans to further grow the Golden Friends business, Mr. Nair promises that we will continue to see exciting products based on the jobs the innovation team has uncovered.

CHAPTER SUMMARY

The tricky thing about value is that it's not a constant. At the same time that a new solution is creating value for the customer, the business must also determine how that same solution creates value for the organization. And both stakeholders have unique concerns. For the business, the first issue is how much potential exists. Does satisfying a job have the potential to impact the company's bottom line? Even if the answer is yes, the company also has to figure out how it can create a sustainable model for bringing in profits over time. From the customer's perspective, value relates to how expensive that solution can be. Does the new solution satisfy jobs or alleviate pain points in such a way that it warrants a purchase? By exploring insights from the entirety of the Jobs Atlas and understanding the relationships among those insights, companies can understand both sides of that value dilemma in a way that moves beyond traditional product sales benchmarks.

You can better understand how much money is at stake with respect to a new solution by framing markets in terms of jobs, not products. Learning about the jobs customers are looking to satisfy and the pain points they're looking to alleviate can help you more accurately size markets, and it can ultimately help you expand that market potential by illuminating new customer types that were previously overlooked.

Basic cost-plus pricing, though common, isn't always a good fit with a company's strategic goals. Discover how expensive an offering can be by adopting a value-based pricing strategy that accounts for the unique or emotional jobs your product satisfies.

Create a business model that allows you to sustainably capture value while simultaneously offering the customer a differentiated solution. Ask questions early that allow you to spot potential risks in your business model, especially with respect to how you'll attract new customers, keep those customers, and ultimately grow the business.

7

COMPETITION

BECOMING KING OF THE ROAD

AFTER THE SUPER BOWL in February 2013, virtually every business publication had at least one article on the same, simple food item. And it wasn't a new food item either. The confection in question has been around since 1912, and it looks much the same as it did back then. So what hundred-year-old food was making headlines? It was the Oreo. Four minutes into the blackout of the Super Bowl stadium that year, Oreo's "You can still dunk in the dark" tweet immediately began attracting attention and sparking conversations about real-time marketing and the future of social media in consumer goods sales.

While it's hard to say how much of Oreo's growth over the past few years is attributable to its social media campaigns, its expansion into Asian markets, or a combination of other factors, the decision to bring Oreo digital comes from a very important insight. In 2012, the chief marketing officer of Kraft (which owned Oreo at the time) realized that Oreo is an impulse-purchase brand that no longer competes against just other salty snacks and sweet confections.[1] She recognized that a customer waiting in the checkout line at the store is really looking to pass time or find relief from the stress of shopping. Through that competitive lens, the customer is more likely to devote her attention—and her dollars—to the mobile app in her hand than the sleeve of Oreos on the rack.

While many brands have incorporated social media strategies into their marketing plans, Oreo is ahead of the game in realizing that its customers are buying its products to satisfy jobs that can also be fulfilled through other products and services. This is ironic, given that the insight was put forward profoundly by the great management writer Peter Drucker back in 1964:

> The customer rarely buys what the business thinks it sells him. One reason for this is, of course, that nobody pays for a "product." What is paid for is satisfaction. But nobody can make or supply satisfaction as such—at best, only the means to attaining it can be sold and delivered. Because the customer buys satisfaction, all goods and services compete intensively with goods and services that look quite different, seem to serve entirely different functions, are made, distributed, sold differently—but are alternative means for the customer to obtain the same satisfaction.[2]

IN THIS CHAPTER, YOU WILL LEARN:

- Why a traditional view of competition limits long-term success prospects.
- How a Jobs-based lens provides a broader view of competition.
- How areas of nonconsumption can provide both opportunity and risk.
- How you can assess your ability to deliver on jobs versus both traditional and nontraditional competitors.

PROBLEMS WITH THE TRADITIONAL VIEW OF COMPETITION

A few years ago, we were in a meeting with a consumer goods company talking about the way Trader Joe's laid out its product displays. The conversation quickly turned into an assault on how inefficient the design was and how it was violating a number of product display rules that the rest of the industry had learned years ago. For example, the open freezers—while inviting—allowed cold air to escape. And shelves above those open freezers tended to offer nonfrozen goods from completely different product categories. But while the freezer design may have been inefficient and costly, and the organization scheme may have been atypical, the increasing popularity of Trader Joe's (along with its private label products) was undeniably cutting into the company's sales at an alarming rate. And there was nothing to suggest that the trend would change anytime soon.

Companies that fail to challenge the established views of what their industries sell and how they operate miss valuable opportunities and leave themselves vulnerable to potential disruptors. Look at the interior design industry, which has long catered to wealthy clients and priced itself too high for the average new homeowner. Interior designers fight tooth and nail for those clients. And then there's Décor Aid, a New York–based start-up we've worked with that focuses on bringing interior design services to customers who have, until now, been completely ignored by the industry. Décor Aid has used Jobs to be Done principles to understand what jobs people are trying to get done when they move into a new home, apartment, or office, regardless of whether those customers currently consume design services or could reasonably afford what's being offered today. By establishing partnerships with dealers of attractive modern furniture and creating proprietary technology that simplifies and strips cost out of the design process, Décor Aid has been able to undercut the prices of traditional interior design firms, quickly capturing market share from incumbents and attracting customers who used to rely on DIY alternatives. In addition to the traditional design markets of attending to an entire home, the company also targets jobs that were previously unaddressed by the industry, such as refreshing a room or preparing a home for a major event.

Focusing too narrowly on traditional competitors also leads companies to become complacent. They focus narrowly on innovations that sustain the business on its current path, further increasing the likelihood that they'll miss new potential. A few years back, Kraft noticed that it had fallen victim to this kind of complacency. In 2011, the company decided to turn things around with the launch of MiO, a water flavor enhancer that enabled consumers to create their own personal types of water. This was followed by MiO Energy and MiO Fit in the next two years. Prior to launching MiO, Kraft hadn't created a new category since DiGiorno frozen pizza (now owned by Nestlé) in 1995. Its last new beverage brand was Crystal Light (launched in 1988).[3] Kraft was rewarded for its efforts to stave off stagnation: MiO reached $100 million in sales in its first year.

AN ALTERNATE VIEW OF COMPETITION

Looking through a Jobs-based lens provides a different view. Competitors can be any offerings that satisfy the same jobs. Importantly, this means that in different contexts, the field of competitors changes.

To see what we mean, let's think about footwear. What is the competition for a pair of Nike sneakers? If the job is defined as providing comfortable foot support for runners, the competition may well be sneakers from New Balance or Brooks. But what about the people who are trying to accomplish emotional jobs when they buy a pair of sneakers? If the job is expressing individualism, for example, the competition could be a bumper sticker or a radical change in hairstyle. If the job is projecting status, the competition could be a watch. Nike recognizes that its core customers have more jobs than just those of comfort and support in footwear. Nike also recognizes that every time a customer satisfies one of those emotional jobs by visiting the hair salon or buying an expensive watch that customer has less incentive (and less extra cash) to buy a new pair of sneakers. That is why Nike has moved beyond traditional tactics—such as associating athletes with its products—to find new ways to satisfy emotional jobs for customers. NIKEiD, for example, allows customers to design custom shoes by choosing the style, materials, and colors of the shoes. The tagline for the new venture? "Express your identity."

Businesses that take a broad view of competition not only differentiate their products within the market but also broaden the overall market by bringing in spending that traditionally belonged to other industries.

COMPETING AGAINST NONCONSUMPTION

Closely related to the topic of competition is the idea of nonconsumption. As consultants, we often hear of organizations that claim to be the first or only ones doing something. Our first reaction is skepticism. Many of these organizations fall into one of three groups.

The first group is the business that defines what it is doing so narrowly that it creates the superficial appearance of nonconsumption. This type of business does not lack competitors; it has simply put on blinders. A business that operates only on Tuesdays and sells only children's DVDs may be able to claim that it is the only business of its kind, but it still competes with movie retailers, toy stores, playgrounds, and other businesses that satisfy jobs related to entertaining children. Look at the experience of Digital Equipment Corporation, a business that dominated the disappearing industry of minicomputers in the 1990s. As recently as the mid-nineties, it was defining its market segments in terms such as "workstations that cost $6,000–$10,000," even while customers were shifting in droves to the cheaper and more flexible PCs. The company was bought by a PC maker.

The second group is the business that is doing something truly unique in its market but does not recognize that the concept has already been tried elsewhere. This group reminds us of the importance of learning by analogy. We can gain valuable insights by looking at how other organizations have solved product design challenges or satisfied similar jobs in other markets.

TURN ON!
TURN ON!
turn on.
TV
TURN ON.

For example, micro apartments are becoming a popular way to increase affordable urban housing in the United States, especially as people stay single longer, but the concept is hardly considered new in high-population-density locations throughout China and Japan. Companies that are launching new offerings in their markets can often reduce their risks by looking first to similar concepts in other markets.

The third group consists of those with actually new ideas, often as the result of a new or emerging technology. Areas of true nonconsumption can present attractive opportunities for growth, but they can also pose significant risks. Organizations exploring truly new ideas need to identify the reasons for nonconsumption and measure their ability to overcome those factors. When Microsoft launched its WebTV (later MSN TV) in the late 1990s to provide Internet access on televisions, it was by no means pursuing a bad idea. Today's most successful companies have come out with products that are variations on that same theme: Apple TV; Google Chromecast; Amazon Fire TV; smart TVs by electronics leaders such as Samsung, Panasonic, and LG. But it failed for a number of jobs-related reasons, including the fact that it could satisfy no jobs particularly well. Large high-definition TVs weren't around in the late 1990s, and the average tube TV did little to improve the browsing experience. At the same time, dial-up Internet was still the norm, so the experience was painfully slow and unreliable. Today, companies are succeeding in this arena because there is sufficient infrastructure (including bigger TVs, faster Internet, and more Internet content) to satisfy the entertainment and information-seeking jobs that consumers have. Even great ideas may be dependent on underlying infrastructure, behaviors, and other preconditions that need to change prior to mainstream uptake.

STACKING UP AGAINST COMPETITORS

Don't get us wrong. While we see far too many organizations ignoring asymmetric competitors and other threats, we are not suggesting that you ignore your traditional competitors as well! Too much of writing about strategy and innovation focuses on responding to the usual suspects, but it would be foolish not to pay them close attention. One reason we leave competition to the final part of the Jobs Atlas is so that your examination of rivals will be well informed by the other aspects of the Atlas. You'll be able to assess the full-range competitors, including ones that you wouldn't have prioritized had you begun your work with a typical competitive analysis.

There are three principal factors to consider in your competitive assessment:

First, what are your relative **advantages in delivering against key jobs and success criteria**? Procter & Gamble likes to call this the Right to Win. Do you have advantages in proprietary technology, complementary offerings, brand perceptions, customer access, distribution and alliances, or cost structure? If rivals have some advantages, how will you render them moot?

Next, what is your relative **flexibility to adjust plans**? Plenty of large incumbents have been upended by new market entrants (not just start-ups) because the behemoths have been unable to adjust course quickly enough. In our experience, far too many entrants worry about an industry Goliath knocking them off quickly. Outside some fields where that's the modus operandi, such as fashion, the incumbents generally will take a while to notice something different and take longer to do something about it—and even longer to do that something well. This creates an advantage in fast-moving fields, although not everywhere. Some markets will take a much longer time to gestate, so your flexibility isn't as vital. This topic is explored in much more detail in chapters 3 and 6 of Stephen's previous book, *Capturing New Markets.*

Finally, what will be **rivals' impact on marketplace perceptions**? Competitors may be slow to respond effectively, but they can still cause problems. They can price their subpar offerings at rock-bottom levels to force your pricing down as well. Equally, they can resort to the time-honored strategy of sowing FUD—fear, uncertainty, and doubt. Innovations struggle when customers perceive risks in adopting a new solution, even if those risks are unfounded. Industry Goliaths can be quite effective in spreading FUD throughout the marketplace. It's frustrating, and it slows innovation, but it works. Figure out how you will respond.

THIS CHAPTER IN PRACTICE—MARKETING BEYOND YOUR CORE COMPETITION

Darren Coleman, a UK-based expert in brand marketing, recently shared a number of stories about organizations—from banks to real estate sellers to consumer goods companies—that have used Jobs-based strategies to differentiate and grow their brands. His experience spans Europe, the Middle East, and Southeast Asia. One example that stuck out was a prestigious racquets and lifestyle club in the United Kingdom. After engaging in some qualitative research with existing members, the club came to an interesting realization. Upon asking these members what jobs they were trying to get done in their first weeks and months, the club noticed that the answer of "play tennis or squash" was actually showing up much lower on the list than expected.

On one end of the spectrum, members talked about jobs related to staying fit and healthy or enhancing their overall well-being. On the other end of the spectrum, however, a surprising number of members talked about how they joined the club as a way of meeting people. Some were looking for business-oriented networking opportunities. Others were simply looking to meet new friends. Armed with this new knowledge, the club focused on delivering experiences that were specifically designed to satisfy those jobs.

It used its newly created Jobs-oriented experiences to focus its customer segmentation efforts, attract new members, and upsell on its memberships. Furthermore, these efforts helped the club attract premium-brand partners that wanted to expose their brands to the club's high-net-worth membership base. Collectively, these efforts were able to boost the club's financial performance.

CHAPTER SUMMARY

Looking at what the industry is selling—or at how things have always been done—may offer some helpful insights, but it's not the key ingredient for innovation. Organizations need to recognize that they are not simply selling products or services; they are selling ways to get jobs done. Taking a Jobs-based point of view and truly understanding what your customers are trying to get done in their lives increases the number of ways in which you can satisfy your customers, and it lets you do so in ways that set you apart from the competition.

Taking a traditional view of competition—looking simply at what your direct competitors are doing—can limit your long-term prospects. It's important to challenge established views of what an industry sells or how it operates.

Adopting a Jobs-based lens can create a broader view of competition, illuminating more avenues for growth and sharpening your view of where potential disruptors might appear. This approach can also help ensure that your brand staves off complacency and remains fresh as the world evolves.

Areas of nonconsumption—those areas in which your competitors are not already playing—can offer substantial potential but not without some degree of risk. Thoughtful planning can help you understand what those risks might look like before you overinvest.

While a broader industry view is essential, that's not an excuse to ignore traditional competitors. Your Jobs-based insights should prove valuable as you evaluate how your own advantages can set you apart and develop plans for remaining flexible as your industry changes.

Remember that even though industry incumbents may be slow to change, they're still an important force with the ability to impact your expectations related to product quality, price, and functionality.

■ PART II ■

USING JOBS TO BE DONE TO BUILD GREAT IDEAS

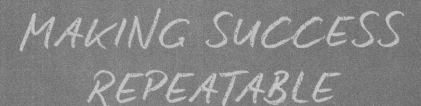

MAKING SUCCESS REPEATABLE

Innovation "silver bullets" are a fiction. There is no single right way to make an organization more innovative. Some companies confine all innovation or growth initiatives to a single unit. Others make innovation part of everyone's job. Many companies employ hybrid models, often having innovation champions who help teams think about ideas in new ways. As long as the approach taken is keenly sensitive to the company's particular context, several techniques can work.

However, there are definitely wrong ways to pursue innovativeness. Here's a big one: Innovation efforts almost always fall flat when they don't follow a defined process. Innovation is not like capturing lightning in a bottle but rather like a competency that has to be deployed over and over again to create breakthrough results. To that end, this section of the book lays out a step-by-step way to move innovation projects forward, using Jobs to be Done as the process cornerstone.

To begin with, innovation projects often fail to move beyond producing intriguing ideas because they lack a strategic compass heading. Everyone may agree on the freshness and creativity of a new idea, but if it doesn't help to move the business toward its five-year objectives, it will likely fall flat. Moreover, it needs to fit with how the organization is cultivating customers, what capabilities the company will have, and the risk tolerance level as well as patience that are credibly in bounds.

Even when innovation projects are given a green light, many die in the early testing phase. Demand simply doesn't materialize. This is often due to an underinvestment in understanding the customer. Design processes that rely on stale or superficial data are not likely to yield products with overwhelming appeal. It is essential to get out of the conference room and talk to real people (not just view statistics) to ensure that you're focusing on what really matters.

Ironically, great ideas can also struggle at the testing phase. A concept that is truly novel tends to focus people's attention on the strangeness of the product rather than on its purpose. People are inherently uncomfortable with what is not familiar, even if it satisfies their underlying jobs. In 1997, for example, Stephen concept-tested flat-screen TVs. Reaction was incredulous: "Why would I hang a TV like a painting?" Similarly, the Swiffer—now a $2 billion brand for Procter & Gamble—failed multiple early concept tests. With the unfamiliar, concept testing must focus on the underlying jobs to be done rather than the product or the idea. Not doing so can lead to a distorted and inaccurate assessment of the potential of future blockbusters.

Once you've scoped your project and conducted research, you should know a lot about your customers. You'll know what jobs they're trying to get done as they go about their days, the hassles they face along the way, and what your solutions will need to do to satisfy them. But you may be left wondering how this ties in with everything else you've learned about innovation. How does it fit with what you may already know about Minimum Viable Products, open innovation, and design thinking? How does it lead to the execution of great ideas? Over the years we've extracted best practices from the leading innovation research—as well as our own experiences—to create an ideation and execution process that can meld into existing innovation workflows or form the basis of a new innovation capability. In this second half of the book, we'll walk you through the process of turning your customer insights into breakthrough innovations.

MAP OF THE SECTION

This section of the book explains how to address the recurring issues that we have raised. The first two chapters—8 and 9—examine what should precede the use of the Jobs Atlas. Chapters 10 through 12 look at what comes after the Jobs Atlas has been deployed. Together, these elements combine with the Jobs Atlas to produce our overall approach to creating great ideas—the Jobs Roadmap.

In Chapter 8, we look at the major questions that need to be answered to determine what a win for the organization looks like, as well as how individual projects can tie clearly into overall strategy and how to find innovative solutions for the right challenges. We provide a number of tools and tactics for scoping projects to give them the best possible chance to succeed.

Chapter 9 drills down into how to create a plan for getting the right answers from customers or end users. We discuss the need for primary research and the available options, including quick, inexpensive ways of gathering information. This chapter also helps you decide whom to talk to when you start your research.

With Chapter 10, we look at structured ways for coming up with great ideas. We don't believe that forcing your team to slog through a long PowerPoint deck of customer insights only then to sit in a room shouting out every idea that comes to mind is a particularly effective approach to ideation, although we've witnessed it far too many times. Instead, we offer a systematic framework that produces diverse ideas, generates meaningful dialogue around them, and ties those concepts to the Jobs Atlas insights.

Chapter 11 illustrates how to bring external perspectives into the innovation process, both to generate fresh ideas and to provide a check on internal assumptions. We highlight ways to fight some of the cognitive biases that may be afflicting your decision-making processes, and we discuss how to take advantage of the trends that may soon upend your industry.

Chapter 12 completes the Jobs Roadmap as we get to the test-and-learn phase. This chapter delves into the essentials of iterative product development, including concept testing, prototyping, and co-creation. We talk through how smart and inexpensive experiments can reduce risks and produce better, customer-centric solutions.

Finally, we conclude with an afterword that looks at institutionalizing the thinking laid out in this book. While many entrepreneurs and project leaders may see the Jobs Roadmap as a careful route for bringing a great new idea to market, established organizations are often looking for a mechanism for continuously bringing new ideas to market. We tell how we helped accomplish exactly that goal with one of the fastest-growing companies in the Fortune 500.

8

ESTABLISH OBJECTIVES

JUST A FEW YEARS ago, there was a lot of buzz in the digital health space, but no one could point to a company actually making profits in the area of health wearables. Companies weren't sure where the money would be, and they debated whether to go after the really sick patients, the well but worried consumers, or the active fitness enthusiasts. Early companies like BodyMedia took a muddled approach and tried to please everyone. When its business suffered as a result, BodyMedia was eventually acquired by Jawbone, largely for its patent portfolio.

Compare the story of BodyMedia to that of Fitbit. Fitbit created a clear strategy from the outset, focusing on a relatively narrow segment of the consumer market: casual exercisers looking to be more active. Rather than looking to radically change the way patients are cared for or force everyone to become an athlete, Fitbit honed in on a very simple proposition—using your everyday activities to improve your overall health. The company keyed in on one overarching job related to easy fitness and offered just enough of a solution to get consumers what they were looking for. It offered a way to track your existing activity levels—in terms that you could both understand and relate to any diet plans you might want to integrate—as well as to set and reach goals for being just a little bit healthier. Despite a very simple model, Fitbit used its targeted strategy to excel. Since launching its first generation of devices in 2009, Fitbit has sold roughly 30 million fitness devices, and it has a market capitalization of nearly $8 billion.[1] Even as the company and its competitors continue to evolve, Fitbit is sticking with a simpler value proposition. In explaining why Fitbit devices continue to outsell other wearables, the company's CEO, James Park, explained that competing devices (such as the Apple Watch) simply try to do too much. Fitbit sold over a million of its new Blaze smartwatches and over a million of its new Alta fitness trackers in just their first month of availability.[2]

IN THIS CHAPTER, YOU WILL LEARN:

- What questions you need to answer to set a strategic course.
- How to craft project mandates that help achieve your strategic objectives.
- How to identify uncertainties that your project will need to address.

SETTING A STRATEGIC COURSE

All organizations—from start-ups to established businesses—need a strategy. While it may seem obvious that a new business needs a strategy so that it can get off the ground, the need for a well-defined strategy is even greater for established businesses. They have to consider how they will fend off potential disruptors, how they will stay

FIVE D'S OF SUCCESSFUL STRATEGY
Define what it means to win
Decide how and with whom you will win
Determine competitive advantages
Defeat specific and articulable challenges
Develop growth options and the capabilities to move forward

Figure 8-1

ahead of existing competitors, and how they will balance optimizing the core business with growing in adjacencies. Deeper than the typical high-level mission statement ("Our goal is to be the market leader. . . ."), your strategy tells you precisely how your organization is going to outperform the competition. Influenced by Procter & Gamble's A. G. Lafley and the University of Toronto's Roger Martin, our thinking on how to develop a winning strategy requires making five discrete choices (see Figure 8-1).[3] Ultimately, your strategy should be an explanation of how your choices meld together to form a concrete plan of action.

Too often, companies fail to get specific in how they answer these questions, or they agree on the easy answers without pushing themselves to go deeper. Successful strategies are ones that challenge conventional wisdom, allowing you to do things that your competitors haven't yet thought to do.

A good strategy matters not just for the overall organization but for individual projects too. With a clearly defined strategic objective, teams using the Jobs Roadmap can ensure that their efforts support well-articulated aims. A major virtue of the Jobs approach is that it is expansive and yields a fully rounded view of latent demand; however, that virtue can turn into a danger of boiling the ocean if there isn't also a way to cleanly prioritize interest areas and determine which insights are most worthy of turning into specific opportunities. Setting strategic objectives, therefore, isn't just for strategy departments; it is for any team looking to use the Jobs approach to produce innovative ideas.

The first step in creating a strategy is *defining what it means to win.* Often this is expressed in the form of a quantitative target (e.g., growing revenue from new products by 20 percent over five years), but it can also be qualitative (e.g., developing a self-serve business model that will allow us to fend off new low-cost entrants). As you define what it means to win, you should also be asking yourself why you have come up with that objective. Why are you pursuing the path you chose? What would be different if you chose a different target or a different time frame? Businesses often announce wild aspirations simply because they sound good (20 percent growth by 2020!) without spending significant time thinking about whether they've chosen the right goals and how their goals can be achieved. As you answer the questions in our model, revisit your initial definition of a win to better understand whether your objectives are attainable and what resources you will need to devote to achieving your goals. And, by all means, never confuse a goal with a strategy—a goal is useful because

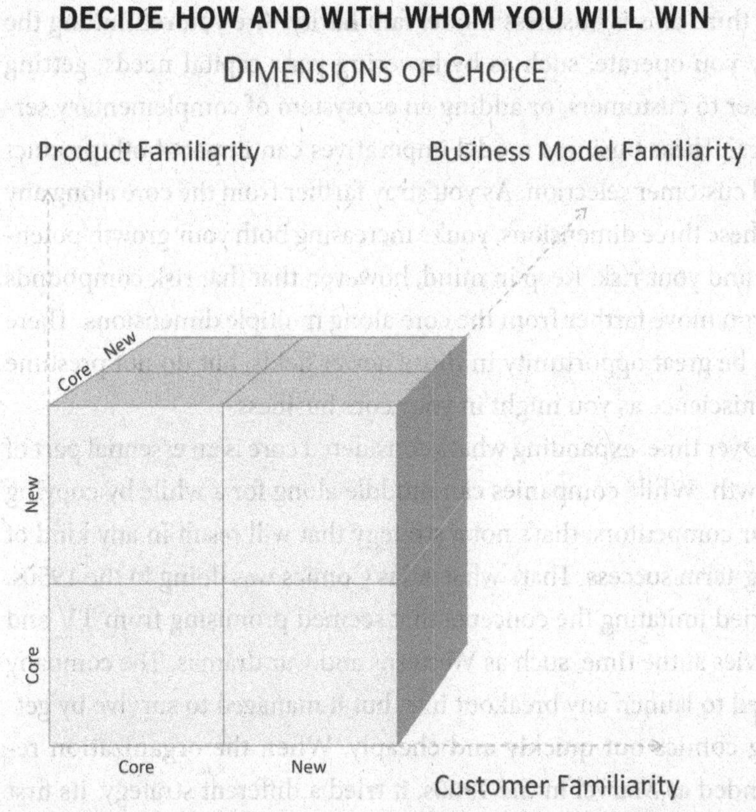
DECIDE HOW AND WITH WHOM YOU WILL WIN
DIMENSIONS OF CHOICE
Product Familiarity
Business Model Familiarity
Core
New
New
Core
Core
New
Customer Familiarity

Figure 8-2

it will impact strategic choices, but it tells the organization very little about what to do or how to make difficult trade-off decisions.

The second step in crafting a strategy is *deciding how and with whom you will win.* Generally this involves making choices along three dimensions (see Figure 8-2). On one axis is your familiarity with the product or service you will be selling. Is this something you've made before, or are you launching into a completely new class of products? On the second axis is your familiarity with the customer you'll be serving. Are you targeting a new customer type or geography, or is the customer similar to ones you've served in the past? On the third axis is business model familiarity. Are you rethinking the way you operate, such as by lowering your capital needs, getting closer to customers, or adding an ecosystem of complementary services? These business model imperatives can impact both product and customer selection. As you stray farther from the core along any of these three dimensions, you're increasing both your growth potential and your risk. Keep in mind, however, that that risk compounds as you move farther from the core along multiple dimensions. There can be great opportunity in those newer fields, but do not presume omniscience as you might in your core business.

Over time, expanding what's considered core is an essential part of growth. While companies can muddle along for a while by copying their competitors, that's not a strategy that will result in any kind of long-term success. That's what Atlas Comics was doing in the 1950s. It tried imitating the concepts that seemed promising from TV and movies at the time, such as Westerns and war dramas. The company failed to launch any breakout hits, but it managed to survive by getting comics out quickly and cheaply. When the organization rebranded as Marvel in the 1960s, it tried a different strategy. Its first step was to take a familiar product—superhero comics—and make them popular again, this time reaching new customers. It then innovated that product; Marvel's Fantastic Four was one of the first to make real-world struggles and adult issues a part of comic book culture, allowing comics to appeal to new customers—adults as well as the traditional younger readers. Marvel continued to add characters with soaring popularity, such as Spider-Man, Hulk, and Wolverine.

In the decades that followed, Marvel experienced pockets of phenomenal success, but it also faced deep competition from rival DC Comics. In an effort to shrug off its financial troubles and keep heroes relevant, Marvel took its core assets—its tried-and-true stories and characters—and brought them into totally new products. Marvel's new movies gave the company's characters mass appeal across customer types. Its 2012 blockbuster *The Avengers* sits as one of the five highest-grossing films of all time, bringing in over $1.5 billion worldwide; it also helped to expose Marvel to still more customers, such as Chinese audiences who hadn't grown up with these characters. It also added more leading female characters over time, such as Jessica Jones, to bring comics beyond their traditional male reader domain. Most recently, Marvel has made a push to try new business models as well. Building on the success of its *Agents of S.H.I.E.L.D.* TV series on ABC, for example, Marvel partnered with Netflix to offer *Daredevil* as exclusive programming for Netflix subscribers. Marvel also experimented with an alternative model for selling comics with its Marvel Digital Unlimited app, which offers readers mobile access to comics on a monthly or yearly subscription basis. While Marvel has seen enormous success by expanding into adjacencies along all three dimensions of growth, it's important to remember that its success was premised on its ability to leverage its core stories and characters—its most valuable assets.

The third step for honing your strategy is *determining your competitive advantages*. This involves identifying the strengths that allow you to expand beyond the core, as well as the assets and tactics that you can use to outperform any competitors who are already playing (or may choose to start playing) in your newly chosen arena. In the ideal scenario, the advantages you leverage will also act as signals to potential rivals to stay out of your new markets. Your advantages will help to determine where to focus, so there may be iteration between steps two and three of this process.

The fourth step for creating a strategy is about *defeating specific and articulable challenges*. It's folly to assume that just because you set a goal you can achieve it. A good strategy maps out the challenges you are likely to face and the uncertainties you need to resolve, articulating a plan for how risks can be reduced and how obstacles can be overcome. We recently talked to Trang Nguyen, the cofounder of Tipsy Art, which is popularizing painting as an evening social event in Vietnam.[4]

While she knew that she could satisfy some of the same jobs as a U.S.-based analogue of this business, called Paint Nite, she also recognized that Hanoi and Boston are completely different markets. For example, she discovered early on that alcohol was a much less significant part of the equation in Vietnam. Participants in many of the early sessions often just discarded their free drinks. The Tipsy Art team quickly restructured around coffee shops, which are much more of a focal point in Vietnamese culture. In addition to increasing demand, this also allowed the business to reduce its drink costs. Even now, the team continues to keep a clear vision of the challenges that will need to be addressed as the business grows, including how to build relationships that will be hard for competitors to copy, how to achieve scale in a business that relies so much on relationships and experiences, and how to ensure that the model is sustainable over the long term even if interest in introductory painting workshops begins to wane.

The fifth step in crafting a strategy involves *developing growth options and the capabilities to move forward.* This step focuses heavily on the "how" of strategy. What competencies do you need to develop in order to gather customer insights, build a culture of innovation, or manage a new business? Your strategy should articulate the institutional capabilities that you will build or strengthen in order to achieve your underlying objectives. At the same time, your strategy should allow for an ability to adapt as uncertainties about the future become clear. This means ensuring early on that the ability to pivot is built into your long-term plans. When a major change or event causes you to shift direction, you should be able to choose a different road, without having to backtrack or blaze an uncharted path through the woods. This is not to be confused with panic! An ability to adapt does not equate to abandoning your chosen course because a new venture proves challenging. Rather, a good strategy allows you to transition to alternative routes when certain predefined circumstances come to pass. You will have already articulated several options and will have a view as to how many of those options remain open to you.

ALIGNING YOUR PROJECT TO YOUR STRATEGY

Once you have a strategy in place, you will need to decide on the scope of the solution space. We often start by making quick yes/maybe/no decisions with some of our initial ideas to sort them into three buckets: the ideal, the imaginable, and the inconceivable.[5]

While we don't want to get attached to any solution at this stage—or even consider that we understand the full spectrum of possible solutions—sorting some early ideas can be a helpful way to understand your organization's boundaries. Are there common characteristics among all of the ideas that are inconceivable? Perhaps they require infrastructure that the organization would never invest in or a change in business model that wouldn't pass muster with regulators. There might also be similarities among the ideal options. Maybe a good number of them leverage a technology that the company has patented. While you don't want to focus too heavily on the ideas you've already come up with before doing any research, having a general idea of what's completely out of scope will help you focus your human and financial resources as you move forward. This exercise also allows the passionate advocates of ideas to get them on the table at the outset, so that the concepts don't keep coming up surreptitiously as you move through the process.

While the next chapter discusses how to construct your research plan in more detail, it's useful at this stage to start thinking about the questions your project will answer. One option is to create a

SAMPLE BUSINESS PLAN ELEMENTS

Market

- What jobs are people trying to get done?
- How big is the market for people with the most important jobs?

Offering

- What does the new offering look like?
- Who is the target customer?

Solution Adoption

- How long will it take to get to launch?
- What will speed / slow adoption of the new offering once it's on the market?

Competition

- Who are the major competitors and what are they doing?
- What are our advantages over others?

Capabilities

- What institutional capabilities need to be built for the new offering?
- What can be borrowed from existing businesses?

Business Model

- How can we create, capture, and deliver value through the new offering?
- What is the financial impact, including costs and revenues?

Figure 8-3

skeleton business plan without any data or conclusions (see Figure 8-3). That is to say, it can be useful to identify the questions you will need to answer without actually trying to answer them at this stage. This means figuring out all the things you will need to prove to the higher-ups in order to get approval for your new solution. In doing so, you will be able to make preliminary hypotheses about what types of research you will need to conduct, how long it will take to answer the key unknowns, and what level of resources you will need to devote—in terms of time, people, and money—to fill in all of the pieces of your final recommendation.

THIS CHAPTER IN PRACTICE—MATCHING PLANNING TO STRATEGY

When we worked with a medical device company a while back, a cross-functional core team had been formed to help advise the company's leadership team on new business opportunities. With some guidance, the team was able to create a compelling strategy that addressed the Five D's. With respect to defining what it meant to win, the company wanted to introduce a new service offering that would have positive operating income within two years and would help protect the company as its product lines became commoditized. In terms of deciding where and with whom it would win, the company was going to target U.S.-based medical facilities that were already using its devices to treat a certain class of chronic patients. For its competitive advantages, the company was able to generate a long list of reasons it could succeed, including its deep relationships with procurement personnel at the target facilities and access to proprietary data. The next step was to map the specific challenges the company would need to defeat, such as finding short-term sources of revenue while they put in place the mechanisms to serve their "end game" customers. Finally, the team developed a list of the capabilities they would need to succeed.

With a strategy in place, the team developed a plan for conducting primary and secondary research. The goal was to develop three models, put them through a competency assessment, then choose a single model to build into a full business plan to present to the leadership team. We plotted out the major questions that needed to be answered to reach that goal, including how large the market was for various types of solutions and whether partners could be used to fill in missing competencies. The core team's early ideas were sorted into three categories, recognizing that there was a distinct advantage in designing a solution around a type of data that the company could access but that would be costly for others to access.

After roughly five months of research and strategizing, we came up with a solution that would help move the company into a hybrid model that would create new service-based revenue streams while opening the door to new pricing models for its products. The solution also created an opportunity to capitalize on several emerging health care trends, such as health insurers paying hospitals for medical outcomes rather than for individual services rendered. By focusing on key tenets around patient empowerment and improving the quality and economics of care, the solution was also easy to market to potential customers.

CHAPTER SUMMARY

Fuzzy objectives and a lack of communication can be major impediments to launching a new offering. The solution starts at the top. Leaders need to create a concrete strategy that answers specific questions—*how winning is defined, which markets to target, what strengths can be leveraged, what challenges need to be overcome, and what capabilities need to be built in order to succeed.* Once that strategy is in place, the teams charged with creating new solutions can decide which questions will need to be resolved and set boundaries on how broad the solution space can be. By ensuring that each step communicates clear objectives and priorities, project teams can help avoid the failures that result from basic misalignment.

Companies need high-level strategies so that they can organize their activities and prioritize how they spend their resources. Strategic objectives are equally useful at the team level, as they provide guidance on which opportunities are most worth pursuing.

Setting a strategic course requires answering fundamental questions about what counts as a win, which markets will be pursued, what strengths and challenges will affect an ability to win, and what capabilities need to be developed.

Project teams can ensure that their work coincides with the answers they need to give to leadership by creating skeleton business plans that identify major uncertainties. Teams should give some thought to which customer types they will target, what the offering will look like, how fast new solutions might be adopted, who the competition might be, what capabilities they'll need to develop, and what high-level business model archetypes make the most sense.

Teams can also ensure that they maintain a reasonable project scope by sorting initial ideas into three categories—the ideal, the imaginable, and the inconceivable—and understanding the characteristics that result in an idea being placed in a particular bucket.

9

PLAN YOUR APPROACH

WITH ALL THE TALK about self-driving cars and connected-home innovations, it would be easy to forget that Google began as just a search engine—and a simple search engine at that. Since the company incorporated in 1998, simplicity has been the hallmark of the Google homepage, which offers little more than a box for search terms and an abundance of empty white space. Yet back in 2000, even with such a straightforward product, Google noticed a problem among its user base. Although people were visiting the site, they weren't searching for anything.

Puzzled by this phenomenon, the company sent a team to a nearby college to do some real-world research. The team discovered that users weren't searching for anything because they were endlessly waiting for the page to finish loading. Used to busy sites with colorful animations and links to other places, many users saw the white page, assumed it hadn't finished loading, and left for other search engines that would load faster. Without the in-person research, Google might have assumed that its simple design was unappealing to users. Instead, it was able to solve the problem with the simplest of fixes—adding a copyright tag to the bottom of the page in order to signal to users that the page had fully loaded.[1] Too often, companies assume they know why customers behave the way they do without actually getting out and talking to customers.

IN THIS CHAPTER, YOU WILL LEARN:

- Why primary research is necessary.
- What primary research methods are available.
- Which customer types to speak with.

WHY WE NEED PRIMARY RESEARCH

A common belief seems to persist that Big Data is the cure to all business ailments. Whenever someone admits that they don't know why something happens, someone else will assuredly suggest that Big Data holds the answer. And, in fairness, data can tell organizations a lot, such as what their customers are buying and whether they are satisfied with their purchases. What Big Data fails to give us is context. It doesn't tell us that the shopper chose a particular brand of toilet paper to placate a screaming toddler who "needs" the one with the puppies on it. It doesn't tell us that although the shopper bought a chest freezer, he plans to retrofit it with his own temperature controls because what he really wants is a refrigerator that doesn't have the built-in shelves and space constraints of the upright models he can find in stores. Indeed, Big Data fails to provide crucial information about why customers make decisions and how they interact with products after they are purchased. It is notoriously bad at telling us how customers emotionally relate to products, how they use them in ways that companies never envisioned, and for how long they have been living with a product's little annoyances, just waiting for a better solution to come around.

Consumer goods companies—and those who generally have interaction with the end users of their products—tend to understand the limitations of Big Data better than most. Companies such as P&G, Dell, and General Motors are well known for having ethnographic researchers on staff. Microsoft is reported to be the second-largest employer of anthropologists in the world.[2] As we explore throughout this book, the benefits of primary research transcend industry and hold just as much value in such fields as financial services, health care, business IT, and a host of other areas across the B2C, B2B, and public sectors. At the end of the day, offering a new solution requires deep insights into how and why decisions are made, what level of frustration will push stakeholders to seek out new offerings, and what criteria new products and services will need to satisfy. Solutions that rely only on aggregated data, without underlying context, simply are not set up to succeed.

WHAT TOOLS ARE AVAILABLE

Companies that aren't used to doing primary research tend to think of focus groups as the primary way of gathering customer insights. To be sure, properly run focus groups can be an excellent way of getting a broad view of the customer landscape, often providing crucial insights that will be further tested and refined as you move toward a finalized new offering. But there are a wealth of other ways to gather these insights as well, with the right choice depending on the stage of the project, your mandate, and the amount of time available.

Many years ago, Roger Berkowitz, CEO of the Boston-based restaurant chain Legal Sea Foods, had requested some information from his management team about the dining experience his customers were having. Afraid that he was receiving a filtered version of the facts, he needed a quick way to assess whether this information was accurate or just what his employees thought he wanted to hear. He pulled together a group of frontline workers who interacted with restaurant patrons on a nightly basis. He didn't hold a formal meeting or ask for a report. He didn't commission a six-month study. He simply got together a few of the people who really knew the business's customers, and he let them talk about what they were seeing at the restaurant. This ad hoc—but highly contextual—way of gathering insights into the customer experience worked out well for Berkowitz. He has now been doing it regularly for the past 17 years.

To suggest that there's one right research technique would be a fallacy. The best research plans involve a mix of methods, balancing the need for breadth of information with fast and inexpensive ways to get just-in-time insights (see Figure 9-1). Testing a quick hunch about customer behavior, for example, might require simply talking to a few dozen customers in a store. On the other hand, detailing the landscape of what jobs customers are trying to get done in their lives might warrant starting with a series of focus groups and in-depth interviews. As we will soon explore more deeply, the right choice of research methods depends on the questions you are attempting to answer.

A few years ago, Absolut—a leading maker of premium vodka and other spirits—began to think deeply about the different settings in which its products were consumed. For the bar and restaurant markets, the company felt good about the level of knowledge it had. Less clear, however, was what happened with vodka that was purchased for house parties. In order to figure out how to best market and sell its spirits to individuals, the company needed to learn what was important to hosts and partygoers. Given the need for context-specific

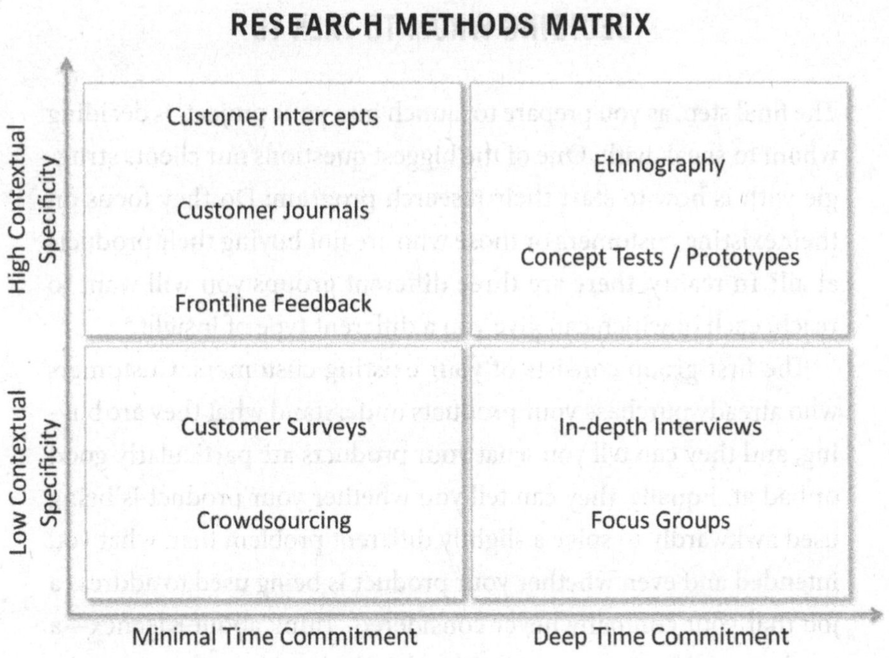
RESEARCH METHODS MATRIX
High Contextual Specificity
Low Contextual Specificity
Customer Intercepts
Customer Journals
Frontline Feedback
Ethnography
Concept Tests / Prototypes
Customer Surveys
Crowdsourcing
In-depth Interviews
Focus Groups
Minimal Time Commitment
Deep Time Commitment

Figure 9-1

insights, Absolut hired researchers to observe drinkers at 18 different house parties across the United States. One insight the company uncovered was that customers weren't just hosts looking for a premium spirit that would impress their guests. In fact, a large portion of vodka purchasers were party guests who wanted to bring a small gift. More importantly, they wanted to bring a story. As it turned out, their purchasing decisions were heavily guided by the narrative that surrounded the drink, not the mark of quality on the bottle. Armed with new high-level insights into the different types of buyers who might be in the retail liquor market, Absolut then turned to quantitative surveys for market sizing and insight validation. Together, these research techniques gave the Absolut team a deep understanding of the retail liquor market, with a human perspective that the team could relate to.[3]

DECIDING WHOM TO TALK TO

The final step, as you prepare to launch into your project, is deciding whom to speak with. One of the biggest questions our clients struggle with is how to start their research program: Do they focus on their existing customers or those who are not buying their products at all? In reality, there are three different groups you will want to reach, each of which can give you a different type of insight.[4]

The first group consists of your existing customers. Customers who already purchase your products understand what they are buying, and they can tell you what your products are particularly good or bad at. Equally, they can tell you whether your product is being used awkwardly to solve a slightly different problem than what you intended and even whether your product is being used to address a job that your company never considered. Think about Kleenex—a product so ubiquitous and intuitive that the brand name conjures an instant image. Obvious, right? Actually, no. In the 1920s, Kleenex tissues were launched as disposable towels for removing makeup. It was thought that they would replace the grimy cold cream removal towels that were hanging in many bathrooms. Their maker eventually discovered, however, that many customers were using the product to blow their noses. The company quickly rebranded the product, and sales increased significantly. As of 2012, Kleenex had a brand value of $3.1 billion and was named by Forbes as one of the World's Most Powerful Brands.[5]

The second group to engage with consists of those customers currently buying competing products. Here, the goal is to learn what really makes those customers different, beyond the superficial answers that they are likely to start with. Look at Walmart, Target, and Kmart—three discount retailers in the United States that cater to very different customer types. Despite a number of similarities in selection and pricing, a quick survey of Target customers reveals that a number of its customers rarely consider shopping at Walmart or Kmart. Target satisfies emotional jobs that the other two do not. Although shoppers at all three stores have a high-priority job related to saving money, Target shoppers tend to be more image conscious. Their lifestyle choices and social groups motivate them to place a higher emphasis on both looking fashionable and buying in a socially responsible way. Through exclusive designer partnerships and ethics-focused product lines, Target has built a brand that aggressively focuses on customers who prioritize such image-based jobs. While Walmart may decide that those kinds of offerings distract from its low-price positioning, it certainly needs to consider these shoppers and understand why they avoid its aisles.

The final group to investigate involves those individuals who are not consuming the types of products you sell at all. Do these customers have a different set of jobs that they are looking to satisfy? Perhaps there is something else holding them back, such as the cost or accessibility of the solution. Regardless of why they are not consuming, these individuals offer valuable opportunities for expansion. And, by definition, your competitors are not winning there either. Let's turn our attention to beer. In recent years, the big breweries have been facing increasing competition from craft brewers and cider makers. Leading brewer Anheuser-Busch sought to attract new customers—those who preferred cocktails to beer—by bringing beer to occasions where it was typically absent. The result was the Bud Light Lime-A-Rita, a product that built a premixed cocktail on the Bud Light Lime platform. The company found that leveraging Bud Light allowed it to make margaritas more approachable and more coed, giving the company a chance to promote an accessible Bud Light product at venues with traditionally low beer sales. This strategy created new occasions for beer consumption. At the same time, the margarita component made the idea of beer more appealing to female customers. While only about 30 percent of Bud Light drinkers are female, women represent around 65 percent of Lime-A-Rita drinkers. Lime-A-Rita sales were over $500 million for its first two years, with over 70 percent of that revenue coming through category expansion.[6]

THIS CHAPTER IN PRACTICE—MEETING CUSTOMERS ON THEIR OWN TURF

When we started our work for a U.S.-based health care provider, we designed a research plan to conduct focus groups to gain a broad understanding of how people in certain cities approached health care. The goal was to figure out how individuals chose a physician, what types of services they regularly took advantage of, and what they thought of our client as a possible site of care.

Qualitative interviews helped show that the target customer wouldn't be defined by income, age, or other demographic variables. Loyalty to their existing physician, interest in alternative therapies like acupuncture, and other factors were attitudinal—and you couldn't find those attitudes listed beside people's names in the phone book. So the follow-on quantitative survey, which needed to gauge factors such as geographic pockets of demand and price sensitivity, required a different approach for finding the target audience. We gathered up our iPads, flew out to our prioritized neighborhoods, and met our target audience on their own turf. We intercepted the people who were exiting spas, natural food stores, and other appropriate establishments. Although we had them fill out a quantitative survey, we were also able to talk to them, observe them, and better understand why they answered survey questions the way they did. Our insights stopped what might have become an expensive foray into a service line that had little demand and instead focused the health system on a differentiated proposition serving a well-defined patient type completely overlooked by preexisting providers in the market.

CHAPTER SUMMARY

Data is a valuable thing. Without context, however, it can also be misleading, and it can prompt organizations to make ill-fated decisions. Organizations that are launching new offerings need to talk to real people and understand the "why" behind the decisions they make. While there is no single best way of gathering customer insights, the best research plans answer specific questions and reduce unnecessary risks.

Primary research is a necessary component for ensuring that you understand the context in which purchasing decisions are made and for learning how products are used once they are in the hands of the end user. While Big Data gives us lots of information about what is being purchased, it doesn't tell us much about why products are being purchased or how those products satisfy important jobs in customers' lives.

A variety of research methods exist, and your approach should be selected based on the stage of the project, the questions you're trying to resolve, and the resources available.

Talking to different customer types—including existing customers, competitors' customers, and nonconsumers—can reveal different types of insights. Talk to all three groups to get a holistic picture of how people choose what to buy or what not to buy.

10

GENERATE IDEAS

BEFORE WE WORK WITH clients to generate new ideas, we often show them an old AirTran Airways commercial that epitomizes the wrong way to brainstorm.[1] In the commercial, a "facilitator" prompts the team to come up with ideas for what they should be putting in their vending machines. The team sits around a table shouting out uninspired ideas, anchoring immediately on the initial ideas of chips and crackers. The only unique idea is also the worst idea—toast—and it results only in humiliation for the proposer. The commercial ends with a man raising his hand to make his only contribution: "You had me fly in for this?"

People often debate whether brainstorming is an effective way to generate new ideas. Unfortunately, many people we talk to have only participated in poorly run brainstorming sessions—those that look eerily similar to the session in the AirTran commercial. An inexperienced facilitator throws out a generic prompt about what the next big solution should be, a few people shout out a lot of not-so-novel ideas, and most people sit quietly wondering when they can get back to work. The only unique ideas that surface are those that the organization will never implement. Moreover, ideas get reduced to a few words on a flipchart, and the discussion and context are quickly forgotten. Then somebody looks at the flipchart a week later and is truly baffled about what might have gone on in that meeting room.

Luckily, the groundwork for better brainstorming has already been laid. In the course of constructing your Jobs Atlas, you've likely started to come up with new ideas already. In fact, if you've really seen the world through customers' eyes, the new solutions may appear obvious, save for the fact that no one has ever created them before. Over the next few pages, we'll take a more in-depth look at how to use the insights you've gathered to hold targeted idea generation sessions that produce promising new concepts.

IN THIS CHAPTER, YOU WILL LEARN:

- Why traditional brainstorming efforts fall flat.
- How simple strategies can help you generate better ideas.
- How the Jobs Atlas can be used to vet the solutions you've come up with.

THE WRONG WAY TO GENERATE NEW IDEAS

Brainstorming sessions are often doomed from the start. From who's invited to the structure of the session, most brainstorming meetings are actually set up—albeit unintentionally—to quash creativity. For starters, boss-led ideation tends to produce fewer original ideas. In those situations, team members worry that ideas that seem too crazy won't be respected, so they volunteer safe ideas and those that they think their boss wants to hear. People throw out the easy answers—those that every competitor has likely come up with as well.

To expand on the problem, those early uninspired ideas are likely to dominate the conversation. That's for two reasons. First, it's extremely difficult to come up with new ideas while you're preoccupied with listening to and evaluating the ideas that others are presenting. Second, we have a psychological tendency to anchor our thinking around the first ideas we hear. Those safe ideas that were thrown out first have now unintentionally established boundaries for how innovative future ideas will be.

To illustrate the problem, what would happen if we asked you to come up with a list of five different tools? We'll help you out by suggesting a hammer as an example of a tool, though that shouldn't be one of your five. What does your list look like? Most likely it contains at least a few other small tools used for building. Perhaps a screwdriver, a wrench, some pliers, or a saw made the list. Maybe, as you struggled for ideas, you branched into power tools. Rarely, with this exercise, do people consider tools from other professions. If instead of an easy answer (the hammer) we had given you a targeted prompt designed to widen your lens ("What are the tools that artists, educators, and accountants use to do their jobs?"), your list would look very different. Importantly, it would also look very different from anyone else's list.

When a facilitator simply asks for ideas and the first ideas are safe and unoriginal, the tone has been set. One researcher found that by having people record several ideas on their own first—without being influenced by ideas from others—groups generated 20 percent more ideas and 42 percent more original ideas.[2] In the next section, we'll look at ways to harvest the power of the group, while avoiding the problems described above.

One other fallacy of brainstorming is to push for overall quantity of ideas.[3] Clearly just having one or two ideas isn't likely to cut it. However, don't mimic the example of a convenience store chain that once approached us asking for a daylong session in which they would generate 2,000 ideas. Honestly? Those ideas were likely going to be incredibly incremental and shallow. Plus, no organization is going to implement anything close to 2,000 ideas, ever. Creativity can be a lazy human function, so it needs to be pushed. Consider only what's realistic and useful.

STRATEGIES FOR BETTER BRAINSTORMING

One of the easiest (and often overlooked) ways of improving the quality of your ideation sessions is to be clear up front about why you're brainstorming, how ideas will be evaluated, and how far flung ideas can be. Companies often worry that by setting up strict rules, they'll be limiting creativity. Instead of setting boundaries, they tell everyone to think outside the box. Worse, they throw open the doors to the whole organization, asking for a flood of new ideas. While the intention is respectable, the outcome is unfortunate. Ideas that the organization would never implement are collected and ignored, ultimately demoralizing those who submitted what they thought were good ideas. While you don't want to judge ideas early on, be clear about what's realistically going to be considered. Are you just looking for new product ideas, or are business model innovations also in scope? Are acquisitions and partnerships on the table, or do new ideas need to leverage existing assets or those that can be developed in-house?

In addition to this early guidance, a good facilitator will focus ideation discussions around specific questions and challenges. Don't just ask everyone for new ideas; you'll get concepts that lack context beyond what proposers already know in their own daily work. An insidious result of that approach—invisible but harmful—is that what might be a big idea is made to sound small. Rather, tie your discussions to the insights in your Jobs Atlas. Ask for ideas on how to satisfy important jobs or eliminate relevant pain points.

Inexperienced facilitators try to stimulate creativity by creating ridiculous scenarios ("How would your ideas be different if the Earth had no gravity?"). These tactics tend to leave participants frustrated, and they rarely produce better ideas. Instead, use the common job drivers you've uncovered to think about how different customer types would react to certain products or problems. Consider how you can overcome obstacles that are particularly onerous for some customers. Your Jobs Atlas can provide a wealth of prompts to stimulate further discussion about relevant concerns.

After you've come up with a few targeted questions to ideate around—and remember that you can introduce additional prompts after some ideas have begun to surface—here are the steps to follow for a better outcome:

Start off by getting everyone on the same page. Explain the purpose of the ideation session, discuss the boundaries of what will or will not be considered, and elaborate on how ideas will be evaluated. It's also important to choose the right setting for ideation. Try to choose a location with an energetic vibe. We often look for smaller spaces where people can actively converse with each other without feeling like they're onstage. Keep in mind that you may want access to additional nearby spaces that can be used for breakout sessions.

Give participants some time to quietly reflect and ideate on their own. Ask participants to come up with their own lists of ideas first, thus avoiding the anchoring problems just described. Give them a quota in order to encourage them to push themselves.

Depending on how many people are present, break the group into small teams of people with dissimilar backgrounds to discuss and expand on these ideas, coming up with new ideas and identifying which ideas seem to have the highest potential. Have someone in the group meticulously record the details of the conversation, as this often encourages team members to think more deeply, and it provides something tangible that can be referenced later.

Once all the participants have shared their ideas, you can group similar ideas together. This will help to highlight important themes that run through multiple ideas, and it will also help to focus the discussion on a smaller number of topics. It's often helpful to separate the ideation portion from the organization and prioritization, such as with a lunch break or even a break for the day. Having a bit of time off gives everyone a chance to gain some perspective, think more critically about their most recent ideas, and better understand the relationships among ideas.

At this stage, it might be a good time to discuss what's on the table. Without being overly limiting, question whether any of the ideas are too far out of scope. More importantly, spend some time identifying the big questions everyone has about the ideas you've generated.

Before you evaluate these ideas, break into groups and build out your ideas in more detail. While you're not expected to build the business case for your preliminary ideas, create a one-page visual that helps highlight why the idea is a good one:

- What jobs are satisfied and what pain points are eliminated?
- What customer types would be interested in the idea?
- How does the idea create value for the business?
- How does the idea satisfy the major criteria identified at the start of the ideation session?

Once you've built out each idea, you'll be able to have a more informed discussion about the merits of the ideas, rather than simply eliminating ideas based on gut reaction. It's important to ask the more senior team members to hold their opinions until others have had a chance to express themselves. If the actual evaluation and selection of ideas will be done by a more senior group later on, it may be wise to avoid voting on ideas within the ideation group, thus avoiding a scenario where project teams and leadership have reached different outcomes.

Finally, as you prepare to leave your brainstorming session, be clear about what the next steps are. Are the ideas going to be presented to senior management? Will there be a full vetting process with a larger group? Does a business case need to be prepared for the best ideas? Rather than leaving team members wondering, be clear about what needs to happen and who will be responsible for moving ideas forward. Without clear ownership, even the best ideas are likely to die in limbo. See Figure 10-1 for a quick overview.

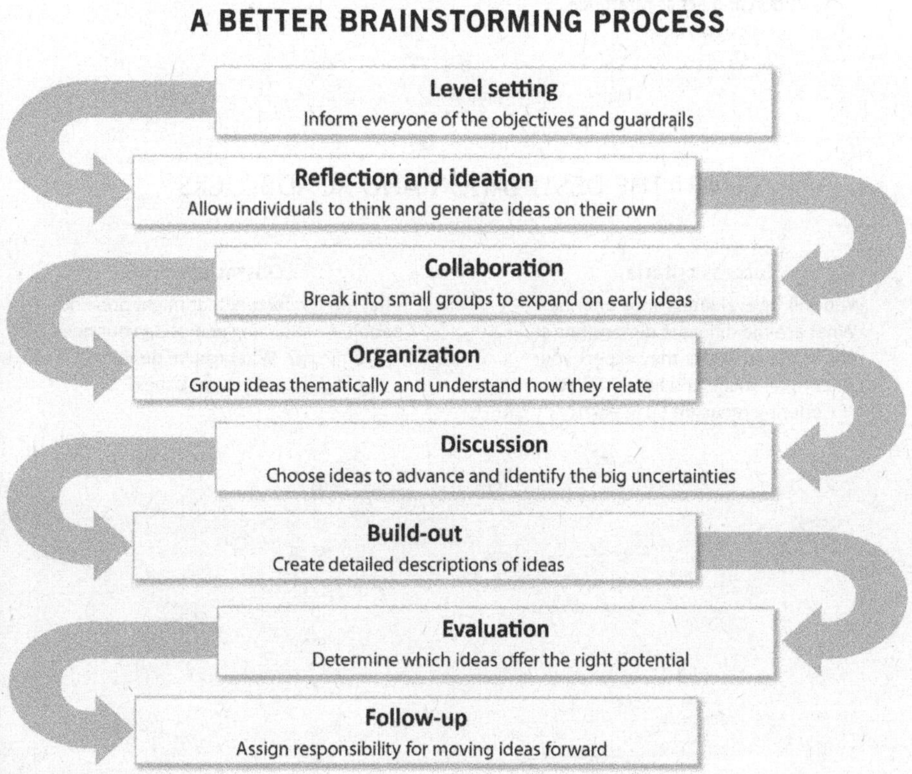
A BETTER BRAINSTORMING PROCESS
Level setting
Inform everyone of the objectives and guardrails
Reflection and ideation
Allow individuals to think and generate ideas on their own
Collaboration
Break into small groups to expand on early ideas
Organization
Group ideas thematically and understand how they relate
Discussion
Choose ideas to advance and identify the big uncertainties
Build-out
Create detailed descriptions of ideas
Evaluation
Determine which ideas offer the right potential
Follow-up
Assign responsibility for moving ideas forward

Figure 10-1

VETTING IDEAS WITH THE JOBS ATLAS

KNOW WHERE YOU'RE STARTING FROM

Jobs

What are the real jobs your solution will help people get done in their lives? How dissatisfied are people with their current ability to get those jobs done?

Current approaches

Does your solution fit with existing customer behavior, or will people need to change the way they act to use your solution?

Job drivers

What subset of the population is your solution aimed at? Is there a good foothold group that can try your solution and act as reference customers?

Pain points

Does your solution alleviate any existing pain points? Does it create new ones?

CHART THE DESTINATION AND ROADBLOCKS

Success criteria

Who will be evaluating your offering? What are the different dimensions of performance where they expect your offering to excel, and how does your offering measure up in each?

Obstacles

What are the factors that might prevent people from buying and using your new offering? What can be done to overcome those issues?

VETTING IDEAS WITH THE JOBS ATLAS

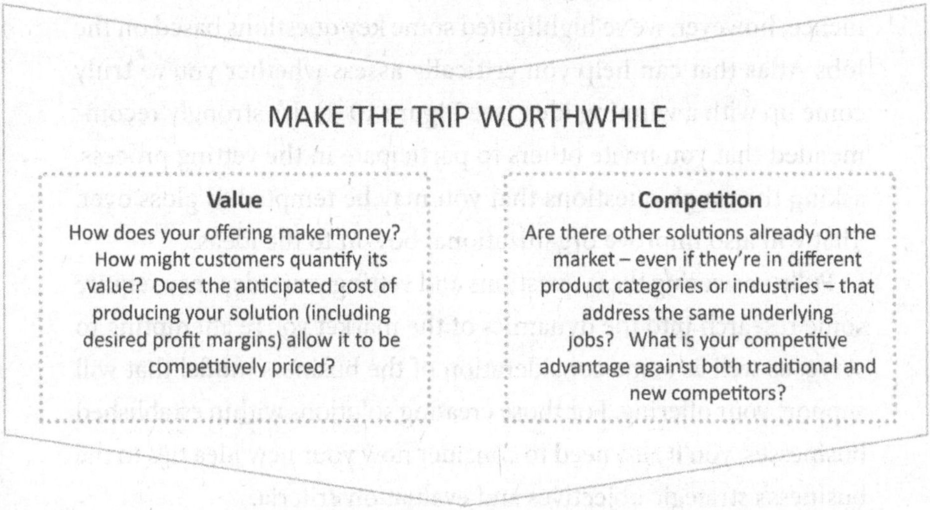
MAKE THE TRIP WORTHWHILE
Value
How does your offering make money? How might customers quantify its value? Does the anticipated cost of producing your solution (including desired profit margins) allow it to be competitively priced?
Competition
Are there other solutions already on the market – even if they're in different product categories or industries – that address the same underlying jobs? What is your competitive advantage against both traditional and new competitors?

Figure 10-2

VETTING YOUR NEW IDEAS

Once you've come up with a new idea, it's easy to fall in love with it. From entrepreneurs to executives, everyone has a great idea that has passed the "I'd buy it" test. Yet as we've shown, most new ideas don't succeed. Assuming you've been following the steps we've laid out in this book, you're probably well on your way to some great ideas. But maybe you're jumping in late and already have some ideas in mind. Or perhaps you've brainstormed some ideas and want to think through them before you evaluate them against your organization's new business criteria. Whatever the case, it's useful to know that the Jobs Atlas—in addition to being a tool for gathering customer and market insights—also provides a framework for vetting existing ideas.

Each of the eight categories in the Jobs Atlas can be used to help evaluate an idea you're considering. It may be helpful to review the chapter summaries for each element of the framework to see how your idea matches up against the lessons we shared. For convenience, however, we've highlighted some key questions based on the Jobs Atlas that can help you critically assess whether you've truly come up with a winning idea (see Figure 10-2). It's strongly recommended that you invite others to participate in the vetting process, asking the tough questions that you may be tempted to gloss over. That will also improve organizational buy-in to the ideas.

Fully answering these questions and vetting your idea may require some research into the dynamics of the market you're attempting to serve, as well as some consideration of the business model that will support your offering. For those creating solutions within established businesses, you'll also need to consider how your new idea ties to the business's strategic objectives and evaluation criteria.

THIS CHAPTER IN PRACTICE— GENERATING IDEAS THE RIGHT WAY

A client once called us and asked for our help leading an ideation workshop. The goal was to help identify and select growth opportunities outside the core business. Before the workshop, we arranged to have discussions with the organization's leadership team and the individuals who would be participating in the session. We wanted to know what ideas had already been surfacing, but we also wanted a better sense of why we were being invited in. We wanted to learn how ideation had worked in the past, what the results had been, and how folks felt about past efforts.

What we heard was fairly typical; two issues came up repeatedly. First, conversations tended to wander off topic, often turning into repeat discussions of old ideas rather than the exploration of new ideas. Second, some people felt that the "real" decisions were always made by senior leaders outside the sessions without much indication of why the chosen ideas were better.

Knowing that the group would be skeptical, we carefully planned a process that would encourage new ideas and avoid the problems of the past. Well ahead of the workshop, we conducted some research into the dynamics of our client's industry. At our first meeting with the workshop participants, we filled them in on why we were there. We discussed why the organization wanted to explore adjacency growth, how much money it would be investing in the projects that would come out of our session, and how the new opportunities would need to fit into the organization's overall portfolio plan. We then shared some of our earlier research and had a discussion on what it meant for the organization. When the conversation began to drift into a discussion about the past, we put those topics onto a "parking lot" list so that the team could discuss them in more depth after the session.

Eventually, it was time to come up with ideas. We talked the participants through a few scenarios based on what we knew about industry trends, key competitors, and customer demands. For each scenario, we asked the participants to individually write down some ideas for how the organization could respond. At the end, we compiled all the ideas, grouped them into themes, and shared the full collection with the group. Discussion of the ideas yielded new options, which we added to the collection. We broke for the day to give everyone some time to reflect.

At our next session, we used stickers to vote—with relative anonymity—on the ideas. Each person had five stickers to put on their top ideas. The group seemed happy with the results, because they had thoroughly bought into the process being used. We then split the participants into breakout groups, each of which was given two or three ideas to build out in detail. Each team was also given a series of questions to answer. They recorded detailed responses that could be shared with future project teams, and they also prepared one-pagers to facilitate sharing the built-out idea with the group. Senior leadership ultimately chose a few of the ideas to advance, reporting back to the group why each idea was or wasn't selected.

Sometime later, we followed up with the client to see how things were progressing. Not only was the ideation team more satisfied with the process, but the new projects that had come out of the session were generating real excitement organization-wide.

CHAPTER SUMMARY

Bad brainstorming is common but quite avoidable. The key to generating great ideas is following a structured process designed to maximize context sensitivity, creativity, and ruthless prioritization. The best ideation sessions reduce the temptation to go after the low-hanging fruit, instead encouraging people to dig for more innovative ideas. They eliminate the pressures for participants to please their bosses, and they ensure that everyone has an opportunity to participate. By adding structure and guiding the discussion around important topics, ideation can be not just exciting but also productive.

Bad brainstorming sessions occur when only a few people participate, shouting out easy ideas to impress others. Avoid anchoring the discussion around those early, unoriginal ideas. Give everyone a chance to quietly reflect and ideate.

The best ideation experiences follow an eight-step process that involves level setting, reflection and ideation, collaboration, organization, discussion, build-out, evaluation, and follow-up. Start by getting everyone on the same page about why you're there and how ideas will be evaluated. Then provide structured questions, and encourage teams to fully build out their ideas.

Whether you're coming to the table with ideas you've already thought up or you're leaving an ideation session with loads of new ideas, it's important to critically vet those ideas. Beyond looking at whether those ideas are right for the business, use the Jobs Atlas to think about how your ideas reflect customer needs and circumstances.

11

REFRAME YOUR PERSPECTIVE

SINCE IT WAS FOUNDED in 1993, Dyson has grown to become a global brand with over $1 billion in annual revenues. How did it happen? The story largely revolves around the company's founder, James Dyson, who is far from a lifer in the vacuum industry. In fact, his entry into the industry was really the result of immense frustration and a penchant for engineering. In the late 1970s, Dyson was frustrated with the vacuums on the market. Even the best vacuums lost their suction when the bags inside started to get clogged with dust. Rather than sucking up dirt, they mostly pushed it around.

Dyson didn't study the history of vacuums or look for ways to keep vacuum bags cleaner for longer periods of time. Instead, he looked outside the industry. Taking inspiration from an industrial sawmill, which used a cyclonic separator to take dust out of the air, Dyson invented the world's first bagless vacuum.

Business literature is filled with stories of happy accidents, where some executive sees a practice in another industry and finds success by bringing it back to the company. Organizations that repeatedly create breakthrough innovations don't wait around for those instances. Rather, they have institutionalized the practice of bringing outside perspectives into the innovation process. As you continue to think up new ideas and evaluate those that you've already come up with, look for ways to change your perspective about your proposed solutions and the challenges you're tackling.

IN THIS CHAPTER, YOU WILL LEARN:

- How to systematically bring in external perspectives and inspiration.
- How to counteract your own biases and tunnel vision.
- How to adapt your solutions to account for emerging trends in your industry.

CONSISTENTLY BRINGING IN OUTSIDE IDEAS

Many of the world's largest companies have found ways to systematically bring in outside thinking. In large part, this is out of necessity. If you have a company with $20 billion in annual revenue (which is below the mean for the Fortune 500), achieving 5 percent organic growth requires bringing in $1 billion in new revenue each year. That's the equivalent of creating a new company—and a large one at that. With a task that daunting, happenstance isn't a viable way to find growth opportunities. Over time, as the internal well begins to run dry, a consistent source of fresh perspectives can be a valuable way to bring in new ideas and new ways of thinking.

Beyond being a source of new ideas, outsiders can also help reimagine and vet the ideas you already have. Once you have an idea on the table, bringing it to others outside your field can be helpful for a few reasons. First, they can provide an unbiased opinion on how new the idea really seems. For those who don't understand the technical magnificence of what you've accomplished, does the idea really seem innovative? Second, they can suggest alterations that are common outside your industry but that may never have occurred to you. IKEA's business model depends on its ability to sell sturdy, lightweight furniture that can be flat-packed. Yet the idea for the cost-effective board-on-frame construction method that underlies several IKEA products wasn't conceived of until a product developer brought back the idea after touring a door factory. Third, outsiders can help you understand whether you're clearly explaining the idea to someone who doesn't live and breathe your internal lingo. While the benefits of your new solution may seem obvious to you, see whether your 30-second pitch can pique an outsider's interest.

The benefits of seeking outside perspectives are clear. But how do you actually do it? More importantly, how do you make sure it's done routinely? There are two ways to institutionalize the practice of bringing in outside views. The first is with an *open innovation* program that establishes permanent channels for reaching out to experts, customers, and other thought partners. These programs are useful both for bringing in new ideas and for generally staying abreast of trends and innovations in other industries. 3M regularly sends its employees out to interact with other business units, outside experts, and customers. A few years back, when the abrasives division introduced its new self-sharpening sandpaper, it used seven different technologies to create the product. Only two of those actually came from the division itself. The rest came to the division through the company's open innovation program.[1]

The second way to shake up your perspective is less involved. It simply requires opening the discussion to people with diverse experiences. When you're planning an ideation session or even just having discussions about a challenge, consider what people from other departments or companies might be able to add. Some groups even institutionalize this into their hiring practices. Corning's Exploratory Markets and Technologies Group, for example, was known for hiring only individuals who had worked with multiple technologies in at least two different industries.[2] Whatever approach you choose, make sure that your new ideas have at least been looked at by those other than the group that came up with them.

COUNTERACTING BIASES AND KNOWLEDGE GAPS

As you come up with and advance new ideas, it's important to pay attention to any blind spots that may affect the decision-making process. There are a wealth of books and articles on cognitive biases out there. We won't attempt to cover all of the potential pitfalls in this short section, but we will look at a few of the more common—and problematic—biases that you're likely to encounter.

As teams try to come up with new product ideas, troubling biases tend to arise from two major sources: the availability of information and confidence in that information. On the availability side, individuals tend to overvalue the evidence they already have on hand. They may rely on anecdotes, personal experiences, and old data rather than seeking fresh customer insights. For example, when we worked with a national retailer to refine its e-commerce strategy, there was a widely held belief throughout the organization that its customers were reluctant to shop online and have the company's products shipped to their homes and left outside. Despite the rationales that supported the idea, there were some within the organization who didn't buy it. They asked us to test the idea further. We surveyed thousands of customers to get their thoughts on online shopping in this category, and the data told a very clear story. Only 4 percent of the company's target customers were uncomfortable with the idea of having the products in question left outside. The customers who may have been uncomfortable had generally developed workarounds, such as having products shipped to their offices or left with a neighbor. By fighting the tendency to fall back on less reliable (but immediately available) data, the retailer was able to eliminate a major perceived hurdle to expanding its e-commerce business.

Also on the availability side, people tend to place the greatest value on the information they get first or the information they've seen most recently. So for those conducting focus groups with dozens or hundreds of customers, for instance, the first and last groups of respondents you talk to are likely to have the most influence on what you take away from your research. Looking back through your notes and taking a count of how many times topics or opinions appeared can be a good way to combat this bias.

On the confidence side, individuals regularly feel more confident in (and otherwise better about) things they've already chosen. This often manifests as people ignoring the faults associated with paths they've chosen while simultaneously overstating the benefits. Relatedly, people tend to seek out information that supports their existing beliefs and ignore information that conflicts with them. The result is that project teams are often flooded with information that proves a point rather than information that presents a balanced view of reality.

So now that we know about some of the important biases, what's to be done? After all, it's hard to recognize and account for biases in the moment. Sure, you can spend extra time thinking about your interpretations and the data that's presented to you, and you can back up qualitative findings with quantitative data. At the end of the day, however, it's important to ensure that you have the processes in place to help reduce the effects of biases before they present themselves. By systematically introducing multiple perspectives into your ideation and vetting process, you can limit or eliminate all of these biases.

UNDERSTANDING THE IMPACT OF TRENDS

We've stressed the importance of looking outside your organization to bring in bold ideas and help you peel off any institutional blinders you may have acquired. Those aren't the only reasons to keep an eye on the outside world, though. Looking beyond your walls helps you

HOTEL
SUSHI
TAPAS
TEX-MEX

spot the trends that are affecting how your customers behave, what else they'll be able to buy, and how the ecosystem that your solution plugs into may be evolving.

Longtime food and beverage executive Christine Dahm helped explain how to tell whether the shifts you're seeing are going to become trends worth acting on. "Trends are different from fads because they're multifaceted. There are two or three different things pointing to their existence, often focused on resolving some of those really important jobs or pain points." By understanding what customers are trying to do, where they're frustrated, and how technologies from across industries are evolving, you'll have a strong grasp on where your own industry will be several years down the road.

Companies that are able to envision the future are better equipped to create breakthrough innovations, but they're also well positioned to make incremental adjustments that can make a big difference to the bottom line. Marriott recently noticed that its one-size-fits-all hotel restaurants—though consistent and reliable—weren't catching the eye of younger travelers. With smartphones able to point out a number of highly rated nearby options, travelers were seeking out specialized local fare, no longer feeling confined to the safe hotel choice. Technology enabled travelers to satisfy the jobs that were important to them—such as patronizing local businesses and trying interesting new flavors—in a way that travelers of years past could not. In response, Marriott departed from traditional industry practices to launch a food and beverage incubator, giving aspiring restauranteurs and bartenders a chance to pitch bold new concepts. Winning start-ups are given up to $50,000, guidance, and a space inside a Marriott hotel. These trendy new locations are designed to help travelers satisfy the jobs that they are starting to fulfill elsewhere, thus keeping valuable meal spending inside the hotel ecosystem.[3]

THIS CHAPTER IN PRACTICE—KEEPING UP WITH SHIFTING MARKET DEMANDS

The Los Angeles company iRise largely established the industry of software visualization, in which IT analysts can create interactive prototypes of how software will function before it is actually coded—a significant improvement over the traditional method of simply keeping lists of desired features. While it continues to lead that industry in many ways today, it saw that the enterprise IT departments it sold to were still struggling with figuring out exactly how their software should function before committing resources to building it. They had largely accepted the need to prototype before development, but they were still struggling to establish a cohesive approach to defining the overall requirements for their software projects. It seemed the underserved jobs to be done were no longer just about prototyping but elsewhere in the process as well.

A focused initiative to understand marketplace trends led to surprising insights. They found that the shift toward using Agile development practices—through which coding occurred in rapidly iterative cycles—combined with the maturing discipline of user experience design and the need to retain some of their traditional list-keeping methods, was conspiring to cause these organizations to comprehensively reexamine how best to define their software projects. As EVP of customer success Stephen Brickley told us, "These organizations were still using a hodge-podge of methods to track their requirements before they used our software. The real underserved jobs were now earlier in the process, as there was an often chaotic process to determine what specifically the software should do."[4] iRise shifted to embrace this opportunity and redoubled its efforts to tie the visualization of software function into a systematic means of tracking requirements. Had it not listened to the market without preconceptions and instead focused as most companies do on validating existing ideas, it likely would not have ended up with this growth opportunity.

CHAPTER SUMMARY

The longer individuals spend at a company, the more faithful they become to the organization's creeds and practices. Creativity may slowly fade away, only to be replaced by excuses like, "That's how we've always done it" or "We tried it before and it didn't work." Inviting outsiders to give input as you go through the innovation process helps bring in fresh ideas and keep those excuses at bay. Furthermore, looking beyond the walls of your organization helps you keep tabs on the emerging trends that are important to your customers, allowing you to stay ahead of what they'll be asking for.

If you're accidentally stumbling across great ideas from other industries, then you're doing it wrong. Achieving even a modest amount of organic growth typically means bringing in substantial sums in new revenues. Your innovation process should have regular ways of bringing in new ideas and outside perspectives.

As you gather customer insights and vet the solutions you come up with, certain biases will naturally affect the decision-making process. Those biases tend to come from overrelying on in-hand information and being overconfident in information that is either deeply entrenched or particularly recent. Adding safety nets to your innovation process and asking outsiders to double-check key assumptions can help ensure that your decisions end up being the right ones.

While open innovation programs can be a good way to bring in new viewpoints and ideas, smaller-scale practices and policies can be just as effective.

Customers expect companies to design products that coincide with current trends. Understanding the new ways that people will be able to satisfy important jobs will help you uncover important trends without relying on a lot of guesswork.

12

EXPERIMENT AND ITERATE

WE'VE ALL HEARD THE saying "No one ever got fired for buying IBM." This expression is indicative of a troubling mindset in business: Safe decisions mean job security. The problem is that safe decisions are not necessarily conducive to innovation. Luckily, more and more businesses are encouraging employees to experiment and embrace smart risks.

For example, in 2014 PepsiCo—the parent company for over a dozen well-known chip brands—decided to launch a high-stakes experiment with its Ruffles brand, opting to spend nearly 100 percent of its ad budget on digital.[1] In 2013, less than 30 percent of the brand's ad spending had been on digital, with most spending going toward TV ads. But PepsiCo realized that its spending, which was based on traditional advertising wisdom, didn't match modern consumer behavior, especially for the company's target demographic. After seeing impressive year-over-year sales growth, the Ruffles experiment helped give PepsiCo the confidence it needed to shift marketing spending away from TV into social and digital in 2015 across its brands.[2]

IN THIS CHAPTER, YOU WILL LEARN:

- How to use experiments to reduce risk and address uncertainties.
- What techniques can be used to assess likely consumer interest in a new offering.
- How customer insights can be worked into the design process.

USING EXPERIMENTS TO RESOLVE UNCERTAINTIES

Experiments sound risky. By their very definition, you don't know what the result will be. Dan Ariely, a renowned professor of behavioral economics at Duke University, explains that businesses often avoid experiments for a very simple reason. As he describes the issue, "We tend to value answers over questions because answers allow us to take action, while questions mean that we need to keep thinking. Never mind that asking good questions and gathering evidence usually guides us to better answers."[3] Used effectively, experiments represent a low-cost way of filling in details related to key unknowns. Will you be able to overcome key technical challenges? Is the idea feasible at scale?

Just because you're using experiments to explore big questions, it doesn't mean that the experiments themselves need to be costly or complicated. For instance, when McDonald's considered adding a shrimp salad to its menu a few years back, a simple thought experiment around scale quickly put an end to the idea—buying shrimp for thousands of its restaurants would have had a significant impact on the overall shrimp supply, driving up the cost of shrimp and making the economics of a shrimp salad infeasible.[4]

Good experiments aren't about grandeur. They're about timing and reliability. With respect to timing, we mean that experiments should test the biggest risks early on. Although these risks may not be the most interesting or the easiest to test, don't get caught in the weeds before you've tested the risks that are outcome determinative.

As to reliability, we mean that the experiment needs to actually test what you think you're testing (see Figure 12-1). While many of us may have thought that high school was the last time we would need to think about the scientific method, its lessons are indispensable. Your experiment should be structured to address an articulable hypothesis, and there should be strict controls to ensure that only one variable is being tested at a time. Look to the experience of executives at the department store Kohl's in 2013, when they were struggling to decrease operating costs. While there was a proposal to open stores an hour later, executives were split on whether this would cause a significant drop in sales.[5] The team designed an experiment

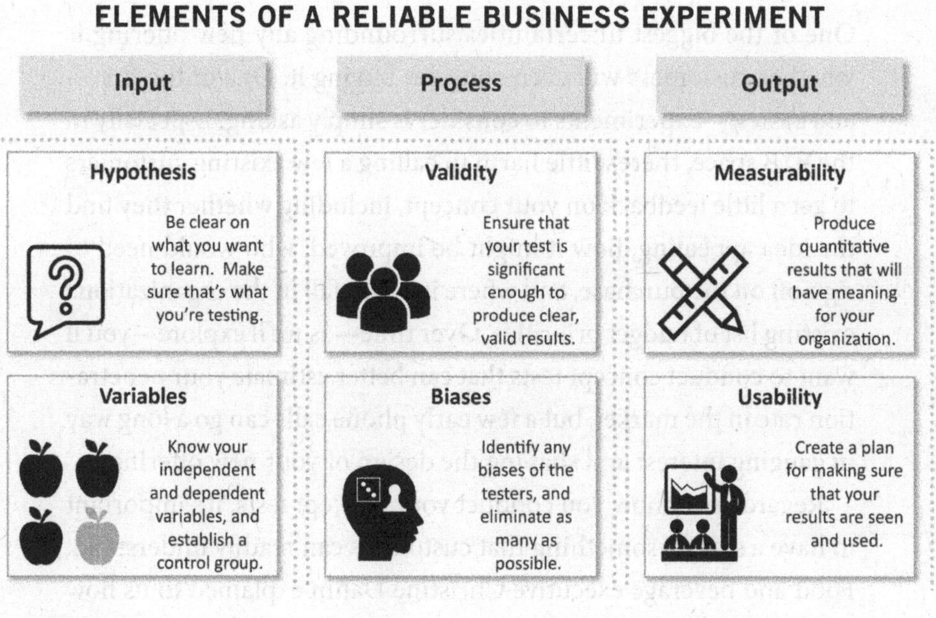
ELEMENTS OF A RELIABLE BUSINESS EXPERIMENT
Input
Process
Output
Hypothesis
Be clear on what you want to learn. Make sure that's what you're testing.
Validity
Ensure that your test is significant enough to produce clear, valid results.
Measurability
Produce quantitative results that will have meaning for your organization.
Variables
Know your independent and dependent variables, and establish a control group.
Biases
Identify any biases of the testers, and eliminate as many as possible.
Usability
Create a plan for making sure that your results are seen and used.

Figure 12-1

involving 100 of the company's stores to test the prediction that opening an hour later Monday through Saturday would not result in a meaningful decline in sales. The test revealed that the impact on sales would be insignificant.

More important than the results of the test, though, was the process. Kohl's made a clear and precise prediction that identified specific dependent and independent variables (as opposed to something like "Changing store hours will not affect our financial performance"). The company also set a meaningful sample size and chose a metric (sales figures) that could be easily compared to on-hand quantitative data. In doing so, Kohl's was able to quickly and inexpensively find an easy way to substantially decrease its operating costs.

GAUGING INTEREST IN A CONCEPT

One of the biggest uncertainties surrounding any new offering is whether customers will even consider buying it. One of the first—and easiest—experiments to consider is simply asking. Especially in the B2B space, there's little harm in calling a few existing customers to get a little feedback on your concept, including whether they find the idea appealing, how it might be improved, who would need to sign off on the purchase, and where it might fall in the organization's existing list of budget priorities. Over time—as we'll explore—you'll want to conduct concept tests that can better estimate your penetration rate in the market, but a few early phone calls can go a long way in gauging interest and shaping the design of your new offering.

Regardless of how you conduct your concept tests, it's important to have a story—something that customers can readily understand. Food and beverage executive Christine Dahm explained to us how one industry powerhouse was exceptionally good at coming up with new product ideas, yet struggled to get reliable consumer feedback prior to launch.

> When we tested the product ideas with consumers, we couldn't re-create the emotional states that the products were responding to. Our tests ended up getting rational responses rather than the responses consumers would have given if they were actually living the experience. We partnered with a TV network to write concepts, and the difference was obvious. They're storytellers, so naturally they were very good at turning our concepts into stories that resonated with the consumer.

As Dahm suggests, it's important that your concept tests help re-create the context in which a decision to purchase or use a product would be made. If you ask consumers about the most important parts of a car, you might well hear from many people that the brakes are most important. If you then ask whether they would be more likely to buy a car with better brakes, the answer would likely be a resounding yes. But when people actually go to buy a car, almost no one is actually making decisions based on brakes. In order for your concept tests to be meaningful, it's essential to create the story that puts customers "in the moment."

This continues to be true as you conduct more rigorous concept tests. As you try to get a better idea of how widely your new offering might be adopted, basic website development tools and unique link generators (such as Goo.gl) can provide an easy and inexpensive way to quantify interest in your concept. Once you've set up a basic web page that tells the story of your new offering, you can take to the streets to hand out cards or brochures with a link to the site, or you can email a list of potential customers and encourage them to learn more by visiting your site. You can track your overall response rate, and you can use unique links to the site to see whether one campaign had a better response rate than another. Beyond seeing who's interested in learning more, your site can use a buy-now button to see how many customers are willing to actually make a purchase, even if (at this stage) the button only takes consumers to a page thanking them for their interest and giving them a chance to learn more when your offering is actually available.

In conducting these broader concept tests, it's still important to pay attention to your experimental design. Remember to think about the number of variables you're changing, the biases that may be in play, and the sample size for your test.

BRINGING CUSTOMERS INTO THE DESIGN PROCESS

The final way experiments should prove useful is in gathering customer feedback. When you look at a new product, the version you see on the shelf is often far removed from the earliest prototypes. As a point of reference, it typically takes Nestlé 100 recipes to arrive at a single new product.[6] Similarly, one of the earliest iPhone prototypes had a 5- × 7-inch screen and was roughly 2 inches thick.[7]

Getting something tangible in front of customers early on in the process can be a great way to gather feedback before you've spent too much money going down a bad path. Early prototypes can be rough, unfinished, and very different from the final product. The point is to understand what the customer likes or dislikes and to capture the questions that are raised (see Figure 12-2). With this feedback, you might make slight refinements to your design, or you may end up going in a completely different direction.

Beyond giving customers something to react to, we often find it helpful to let them help "build" the new offering. In focus groups, for instance, we may have participants design packaging or a mar-

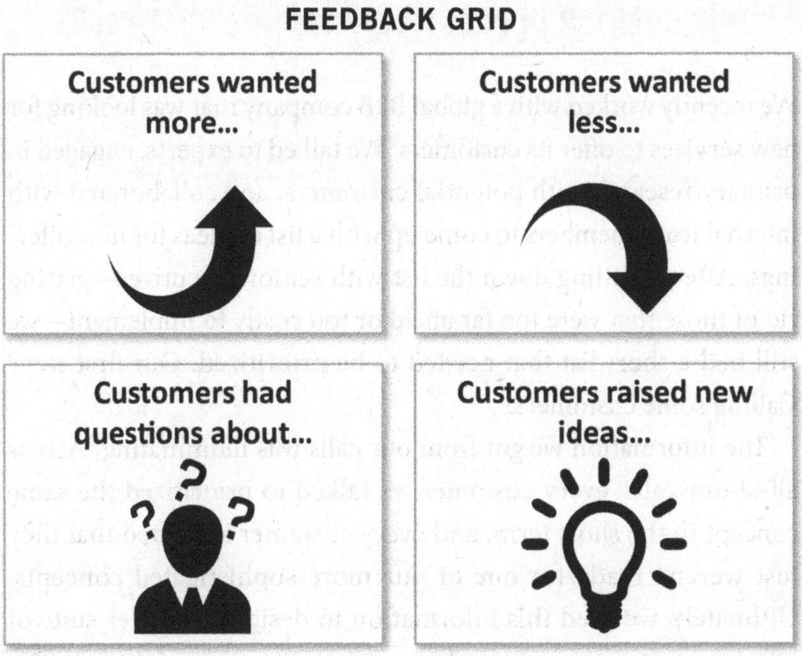
FEEDBACK GRID
Customers wanted more...
Customers wanted less...
Customers had questions about...
Customers raised new ideas...

Figure 12-2

keting poster for a concept that we've come up with during the session. They'll be asked to pitch their finished designs back to us, which gives us a chance to see what features and messaging they focus on, as well as what associations they may make with existing offerings. Similarly, we'll sometimes give participants a set amount of fake money to spend on product features and offer them a limited set of features to buy. The features will have different price points that reflect the relative costs or difficulty associated with actually building in those features. This type of data helps us determine whether the product attributes that we plan on investing in are valuable enough to the consumer to justify the expense. It makes things more genuine than simply asking them what matters, when they may speak rationally but unrealistically.

THIS CHAPTER IN PRACTICE—CALLING CUSTOMERS

We recently worked with a global B2B company that was looking for new services to offer its customers. We talked to experts, engaged in primary research with potential customers, and collaborated with internal team members to come up with a list of ideas for new offerings. After whittling down the list with senior executives—getting rid of those that were too far afield or too costly to implement—we still had a short list that needed to be prioritized. Our first step? Calling some customers.

The information we got from our calls was illuminating. Across all of our calls, every customer we talked to prioritized the same concept in the short term, and every customer indicated that they just weren't ready for one of our more sophisticated concepts. Ultimately, we used this information to design a broader suite of offerings that customers could grow into over time. We were also able to get useful estimates on how we could price the new offerings, how long the decision-making process would take, and where the company's brand was an asset or a hindrance in the sales process. The value we got from our calls far exceeded the value of the hours we spent on the phone.

CHAPTER SUMMARY

Companies—and the individuals running them—tend to be somewhat risk averse. People value answers over questions, so they shy away from experiments, which will necessarily have uncertain results. But the quality of information you can get from targeted experiments can be unparalleled. By running fast, inexpensive experiments that answer key questions, companies can make better informed decisions, substantially reducing the amounts of time and money that are typically wasted on failed innovation efforts. In particular, customer-facing experiments can provide invaluable insights into how customers make decisions, what they're looking for in a new offering, and whether they're likely to consider buying whatever it is you're trying to sell.

Experiments can be an inexpensive way to resolve major unknowns before a project is too far along. Experiments should follow a careful design to ensure that the results are both valid and useful.

Concept tests can be a useful way to determine whether customers are interested in your new offering, but each concept needs a story that helps re-create the experience in which a customer would actually be making a decision to purchase or use the product.

Customers can help shape the design of your final product by reacting to prototypes or participating in activities designed to highlight what's really important to them. Be sure to capture what customers like and dislike, as well as the questions they raise and any new ideas they may propose.

▪ AFTERWORD ▪

INSTITUTIONALIZING JOBS TO BE DONE THINKING

BUILDING THE CAPABILITIES FOR REPEATED SUCCESS

UNDERSTANDING HOW TO USE the Jobs Roadmap to achieve success on a particular project is important. For continued success, however, Jobs to be Done principles need to be accepted more broadly throughout the organization. In 2012, we started working with Cognizant, a B2B technology company that is one of the fastest-growing companies in the Fortune 500. It has made 12 consecutive appearances (2003–2014) on Fortune's 100 Fastest-Growing Companies list. Its revenues grew from just $229 million in 2002 to $10.3 billion in 2014 and have more than doubled in just the past five years (see Figure 13-1).

The fast revenue growth has been accompanied by equally astonishing employee growth. Cognizant now has over 200,000 employees working in roughly 50 countries. While this kind of growth is fantastic, it always comes with challenges. When we began our work with Cognizant, we were asked to help address one challenge in particular: building a uniform structure to help drive customer-centric innovation across the company's decentralized workforce. Not only

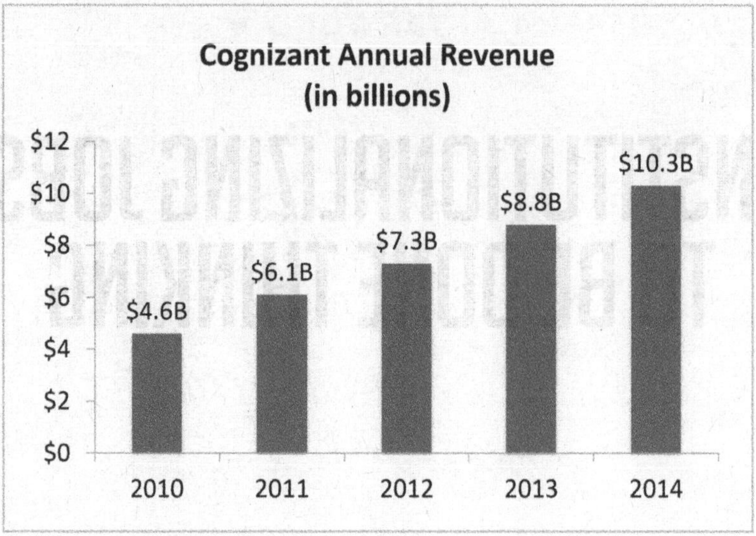
Cognizant Annual Revenue
(in billions)
$12
$10
$8
$6
$4
$2
$0
$4.6B
$6.1B
$7.3B
$8.8B
$10.3B
2010
2011
2012
2013
2014

Figure 13-1

did the work need to create a standard framework that could be applied consistently across the company's global workforce, but it also needed to yield immediate results to ensure that the initiative got enough attention to be properly funded.

Working with the innovation team, we decided on five pillars that would distinguish the Jobs-based innovation initiative from traditional corporate training programs (see Figure 13-2). The first was that the initiative needed to advance ongoing projects and generate immediate value without interrupting employees' "day jobs." To meet that goal, we divided the initial group of participants into small teams. Each team was paired with an account manager, who was asked to bring a current client challenge to our initial workshop. As we helped teams understand the fundamentals of the Jobs Roadmap, we also steadily helped them pick at pieces of the account managers' challenges. The second day of our workshop was devoted to fully solving as much of each challenge as possible, then creating

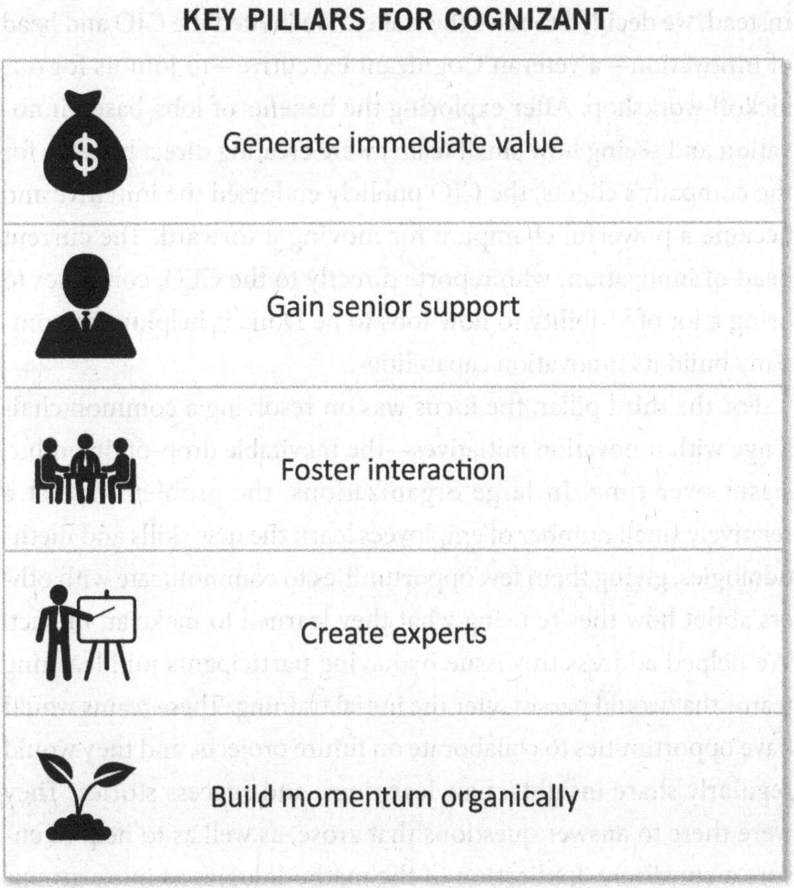
KEY PILLARS FOR COGNIZANT
Generate immediate value
Gain senior support
Foster interaction
Create experts
Build momentum organically

Figure 13-2

clear work plans for issues that needed to be resolved directly with the client. We also left participants with job aids that they could use quickly and easily when they got stuck with future projects.

The second requirement focused on getting senior leadership to support the methodology and encourage its use directly with clients. In such a large workforce, gradually building support by going up the ranks would have killed the momentum we hoped to gain.

Instead, we decided to raise the stakes. We invited the CIO and head of innovation—a veteran Cognizant executive—to join us for our kickoff workshop. After exploring the benefits of Jobs-based innovation and seeing how small teams were creating direct benefits for the company's clients, the CIO publicly endorsed the initiative and became a powerful champion for moving it forward. The current head of innovation, who reports directly to the CEO, continues to bring a lot of visibility to how Jobs to be Done is helping the company build its innovation capabilities.

For the third pillar, the focus was on resolving a common challenge with innovation initiatives—the inevitable drop-off in enthusiasm over time. In large organizations, the problem is that a relatively small number of employees learn the new skills and methodologies, giving them few opportunities to communicate with others about how they're using what they learned to make an impact. We helped address this issue by having participants join learning teams that would persist after the initial training. These teams would have opportunities to collaborate on future projects, and they would regularly share insights, new learnings, and success stories. They were there to answer questions that arose, as well as to help to ensure a consistent application of the methodologies as more groups went through the training initiative.

Our fourth objective was to focus on the creation of internal experts. Even as Cognizant introduced more and more of its employees to Jobs to be Done principles, the company continued to grow. Even if the company could train 10,000 employees per year, it would still take decades to fully train its entire workforce. Instead, we decided to focus on creating experts within the innovation group who would be able to provide just-in-time tools and guidance to project teams who could benefit from Jobs-based learnings. We continued to work with participants who were interested in learning more, ultimately turning them into trusted leaders whom their colleagues now turn to.

The fifth pillar revolved around building momentum organically. As previously hinted at, bringing in consultants to train hundreds of thousands of employees was simply not a viable model. Relatedly, one-and-done training programs don't give employees anything to work toward. Instead, we created a multilevel certification program that encouraged participants to continue applying what they had learned and advance through the program's levels. Then participants who reached the highest level of certification were invited to work with us further so that we could help them get ready to train their colleagues on their own. Not only has this made the initiative scalable, but it has also created a built-in reason for employees to continue using Jobs to be Done principles in their everyday work.

Employees in client-facing roles who went through the program quickly began using what they learned to design IT solutions that better fit their clients' needs. But they were not the only ones to take advantage of the program. Employees with internal roles found ways to use Jobs-based methodologies to improve back-end processes as well. After bringing their learnings back to their departments, they found opportunities to optimize existing processes and improve the experience of working at Cognizant, such as by improving cross-team communication, rethinking employee transit options, designing better hiring and onboarding processes, and streamlining sales protocols. Across the organization, employees were finding myriad ways to make a difference. In 2015, Cognizant was named as one of the world's 100 most innovative companies by Forbes.

TAILORING CAPABILITIES TO SPECIFIC NEEDS AND CULTURES

While the design for Cognizant's innovation initiative fit its needs, it's not the only approach to institutionalizing Jobs-based thinking.

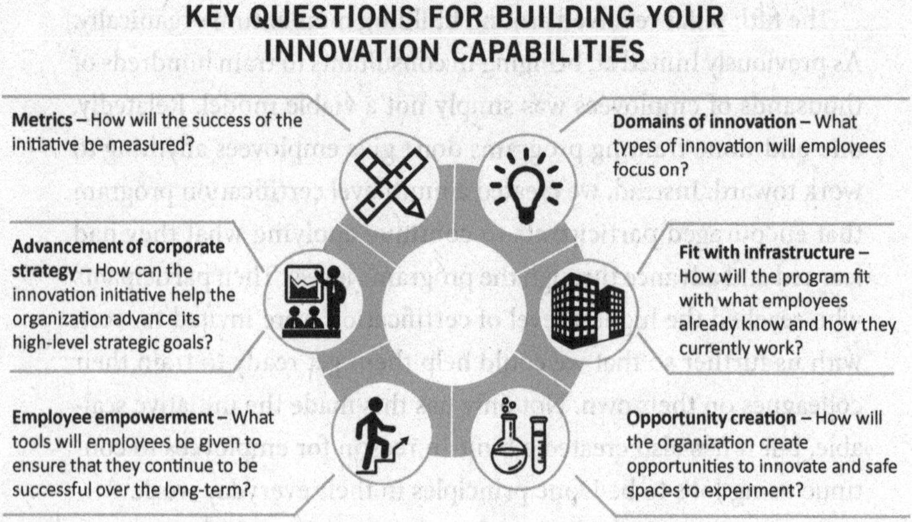
KEY QUESTIONS FOR BUILDING YOUR INNOVATION CAPABILITIES
Metrics – How will the success of the initiative be measured?
Domains of innovation – What types of innovation will employees focus on?
Advancement of corporate strategy – How can the innovation initiative help the organization advance its high-level strategic goals?
Fit with infrastructure – How will the program fit with what employees already know and how they currently work?
Employee empowerment – What tools will employees be given to ensure that they continue to be successful over the long-term?
Opportunity creation – How will the organization create opportunities to innovate and safe spaces to experiment?

Figure 13-3

Cognizant's unique mix of characteristics—rapid growth, a decentralized workforce, and an industry that demands constant innovation—led to the approach we rolled out. But an innovation program is not as simple as purchasing and installing some software. Instead, these initiatives need to account for an organization's growth stage, strategic objectives, and organizational culture.

Over the years, we've helped institute Jobs-based programs to fit a broad range of needs across wildly different industries. As different as the end programs may look, the design process always looks similar (see Figure 13-3). It requires understanding how innovation is currently working (or not working), as well as the cultural and practical constraints that will affect how deeply participants will immerse themselves, how broadly the program will reach, and how content will be delivered and absorbed. At the same time, designing an innovation initiative requires looking to the future to understand how the program will help the organization reach its long-term strategic goals.

Cognizant's program has succeeded because it is staged, multi-threaded, and responsive to the organization's specific context. That sounds sensible, but it's far too uncommon. Once an organization opts for Jobs to be Done as an innovation methodology (or for any other methodology, for that matter), such a focused campaign can drive long-term, meaningful change. Like any effort, it takes work. The payoff can be immense.

■ APPENDIX A ■

QUICK REFERENCE GUIDE

As you conduct your primary research, this quick reference guide is meant to help you remember key points about each element of our framework. Once you've gathered your own insights, you'll be able to analyze the patterns among your data points and ultimately build your own Jobs Atlas around specific customer types, occasions, or other opportunity areas. To clarify some of our key points, we've included examples based on hypothetical customer insights related to weekend snacking occasions for families. Remember that your findings will be highly dependent on context. As you'll see even in our short example, these insights would change significantly if you were looking at different customer types or different consumption occasions. Also note that our examples are meant to be illustrative. They represent only a small snapshot of the insights you would expect to uncover by using our framework to engage in actual primary research.

■ ■ ■

JOBS

REFRESHER POINTS:

- Jobs are the tasks that consumers are trying to get done in their everyday lives.
- Research needs to focus on uncovering consumers' jobs, not just what they're currently buying or what they think a good solution would look like.
- Look to satisfy both functional and emotional jobs.
- While consumers will be looking to satisfy a number of jobs, some will be more important than others. Focus first on satisfying those "North Star" jobs.
- In your research, keep asking "why?" to make sure you understand the true underlying jobs.

Example:

JOBS
Focusing on jobs
Focusing on features
Make sure my family isn't hungry waiting for dinner
Bigger bag of chips
Occupy the children when they get bored
Snack that lasts a while
Reward everyone for having healthy meals all week
More chocolate in my snack

JOB DRIVERS

REFRESHER POINTS:

- Job drivers are the underlying factors that make particular jobs more or less important for different types of consumers.
- Job drivers can be uncovered by looking at three broad categories: attitudes, background, and circumstances.
- Jobs and job drivers combine to yield customer segments—groups of customers who will buy and behave in similar ways.
- Rather than building fully loaded, one-size-fits-none products, new offerings should be targeted to specific customer segments by focusing on the jobs that are important to those specific consumers.

Example:

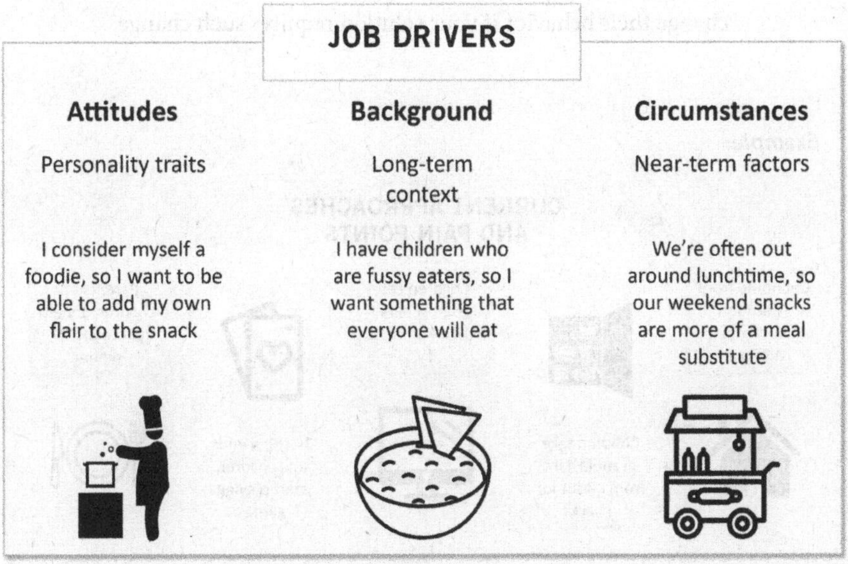
JOB DRIVERS
Attitudes
Personality traits
I consider myself a foodie, so I want to be able to add my own flair to the snack
Background
Long-term context
I have children who are fussy eaters, so I want something that everyone will eat
Circumstances
Near-term factors
We're often out around lunchtime, so our weekend snacks are more of a meal substitute

CURRENT APPROACHES AND PAIN POINTS

REFRESHER POINTS:

- The product purchaser is just one of several stakeholders who may need to be satisfied with your new offering. Consider whether there is an end user or other key decision maker who will need to be satisfied.
- Current approaches are the range of activities that collectively represent a customer's way of doing something. Pain points—a breeding ground for innovation—are the areas of difficulty, frustration, or inefficiency along the way.
- Because context can affect which jobs are in play, remember to ask about specific occasions (not just average behavior), getting as detailed as possible.
- Consumers are often attached to their current approaches, so carefully consider how fast you can expect consumers to change their behavior if your solution requires such change.

Example:

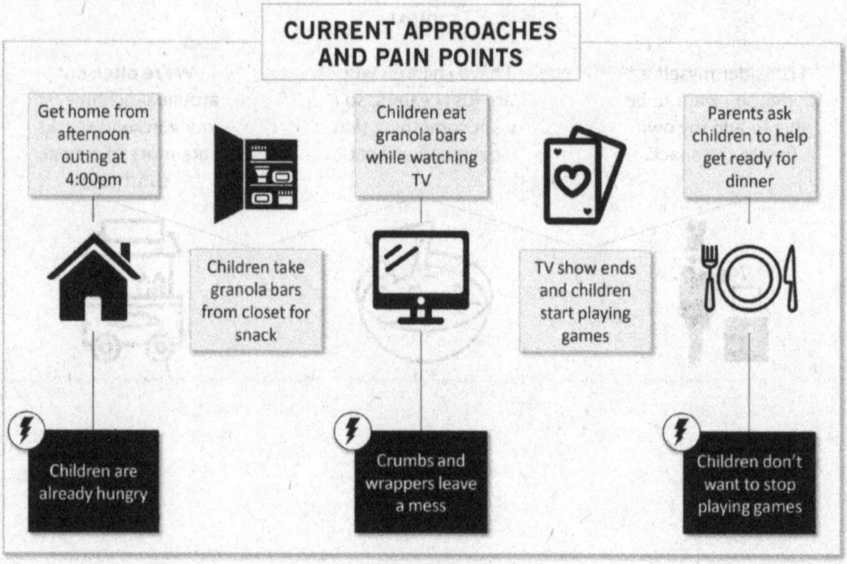
CURRENT APPROACHES AND PAIN POINTS
Get home from afternoon outing at 4:00pm
Children take granola bars from closet for snack
Children eat granola bars while watching TV
TV show ends and children start playing games
Parents ask children to help get ready for dinner
Children are already hungry
Crumbs and wrappers leave a mess
Children don't want to stop playing games

SUCCESS CRITERIA

REFRESHER POINTS:

- Success criteria are not jobs but rather indications of whether a job has been satisfied.
- The success of a new product will often require homing in on particular occasions and contexts that are the most important to the customer.
- To get started, try understanding what customers want more of, what they want less of, and where they're seeking a balance.
- Your new solution may ultimately require making trade-offs. It's perfectly acceptable to give up on features that matter to a limited number of customers as long as you excel along the dimensions that matter most to your targeted customer segments.

Example:

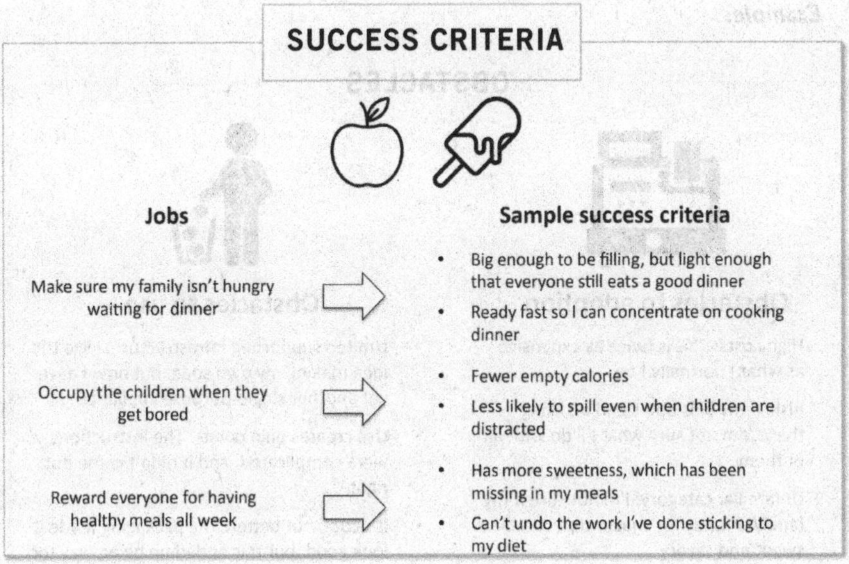
SUCCESS CRITERIA
Jobs
Sample success criteria
Make sure my family isn't hungry waiting for dinner
Big enough to be filling, but light enough that everyone still eats a good dinner
Ready fast so I can concentrate on cooking dinner
Occupy the children when they get bored
Fewer empty calories
Less likely to spill even when children are distracted
Reward everyone for having healthy meals all week
Has more sweetness, which has been missing in my meals
Can't undo the work I've done sticking to my diet

OBSTACLES

REFRESHER POINTS:

- Obstacles come in two forms: obstacles to adoption and obstacles to use.
- Obstacles to adoption are hurdles that limit a consumer's willingness to buy an offering.
- Obstacles to adoption can be reduced by making it easy for people to learn about and try your new offering.
- Obstacles to use are hurdles that get in the way of success, thereby limiting a customer's likelihood of continuing to use a product, purchasing add-ons, or upgrading to newer versions.
- Continuously acquiring a new customer base is often too costly to be sustainable, making it important to eliminate obstacles to use so that first-time buyers become repeat buyers.

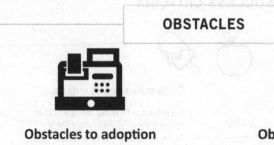

Example:

OBSTACLES

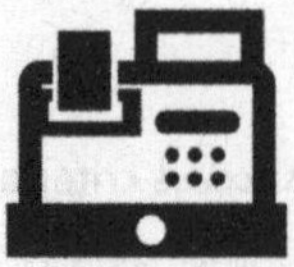

Obstacles to adoption

- High costs: This is twice as expensive as what I normally buy
- Risk: If my kids don't end up liking these, I'm not sure what I'll do with all of them
- Unfamiliar category: I'm not sure if my family is ready for snacks that combine sweet and savory

Obstacles to use

- Limited supporting infrastructure: I like the idea making my own soda, but now I have yet another single-purpose appliance
- Use creates pain points: The instructions were complicated, and it didn't come out right
- It's cool, not better: The packaging made it look good, but this ended up being way too messy to serve to kids

VALUE

REFRESHER POINTS:

- Understanding how much money is at stake with respect to a new solution requires framing markets in terms of jobs, not products.
- A value-based pricing strategy that accounts for the unique or emotional jobs your offering satisfies can help you more accurately understand how expensive your solution can and should be.
- In addition to thinking about the value you're offering the customer and other key stakeholders, your solution needs to bring in value for the organization. Consider whether your model allows you to sustainably capture value.

Example:

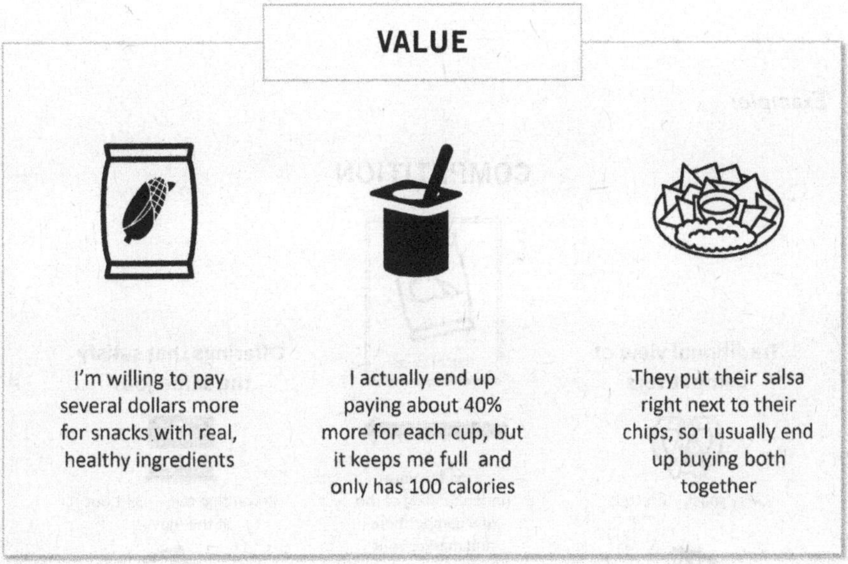
VALUE
I'm willing to pay several dollars more for snacks with real, healthy ingredients
I actually end up paying about 40% more for each cup, but it keeps me full and only has 100 calories
They put their salsa right next to their chips, so I usually end up buying both together

COMPETITION

REFRESHER POINTS:

- Beyond your traditional or direct competitors, your offering also competes against other offerings that satisfy the same jobs.
- Because consumers will look outside your product category to satisfy their jobs to be done, familiarize yourself with the entire spectrum of direct and indirect competitors, and position your products accordingly.
- By applying a Jobs-based lens, your broader view can also illuminate more avenues for growth.
- Areas of nonconsumption—the areas in which your competitors aren't currently playing—can offer substantial potential, but they also carry some degree of risk.
- Think about both traditional and nontraditional competitors in terms of your relative advantages, flexibility, and risk.

Example:

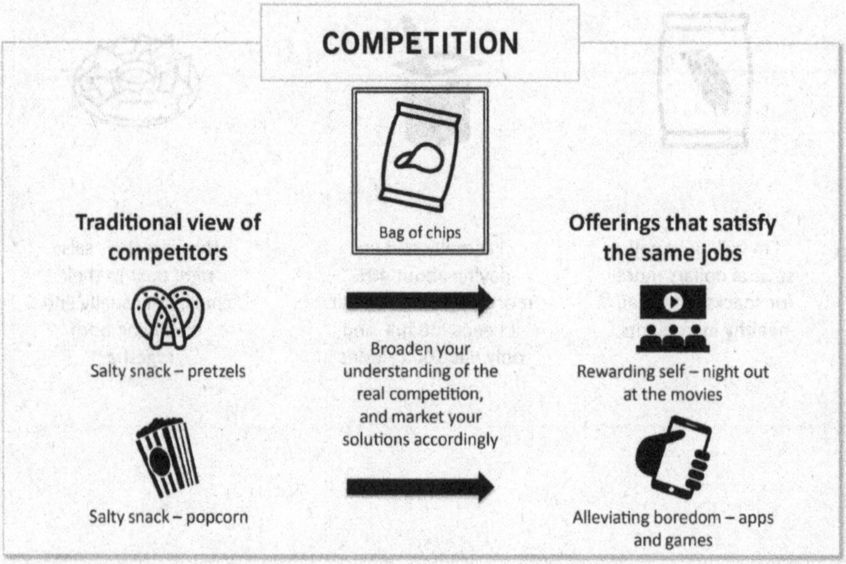
COMPETITION
Bag of chips
Traditional view of competitors
Salty snack – pretzels
Salty snack – popcorn
Broaden your understanding of the real competition, and market your solutions accordingly
Offerings that satisfy the same jobs
Rewarding self – night out at the movies
Alleviating boredom – apps and games

■ APPENDIX B ■

JOBS IN THE PUBLIC SECTOR

International development organizations can be terrible innovators. On the front lines of some of the world's most daunting challenges—large-scale refugee crises, epidemics, environmental disasters—they tend to be startlingly unimaginative in how they approach their work. It's not for lack of effort or talent. Institutions like Oxfam, Save the Children, and Care attract some of the best and brightest individuals from each generation and keep them working in the field for decades. These folks know their stuff and are committed to making an impact.

Rather, the innovation struggle for international charities reflects common problems found in many large organizations, both public and private: a supply-driven assessment of the environment, problems, and opportunities, as well as an overly structured approach to how they operate. These self-imposed constraints doom the majority of development work to remain uninspired and somewhat ineffective. When they do succeed in innovating, it's typically due to one-off factors that are seldom replicated. That's the negative news.

On the positive side, the fix is not difficult and not out of line with how international NGOs and other such actors already define themselves and their social-good missions. Not surprisingly, it involves using Jobs to be Done. Rather than dwelling on the deficiencies of international development groups, we look to illustrations of a better way to work, using these as an example of how these principles apply to the public sector overall.

THE IMPORTANCE OF CONTEXT

For a glimpse at how a rigorous dissection of jobs, current approaches, success criteria, and obstacles can bear fruit, look to the story of a major lifesaving innovation—Plumpy'Nut. André Briend, the French creator of Plumpy'Nut, was frustrated but determined. By the mid-1990s, he had spent years working in humanitarian crises as a pediatric nutritionist, and he had seen the shortcomings of international response. The standard treatment for severe malnutrition was a substance called F-100—a milk powder developed in the 1980s that was fortified with vitamins and minerals. He knew it failed to accomplish key jobs in the context of a crisis. F-100 was not getting to many of the children most in need, nor was it enabling agencies to extend their efforts far into the field.

In humanitarian emergencies, resources are scarce and erratically obtained. Response centers are often overwhelmed by people. Conditions out in the countryside are dire, and transport to and from logistics hubs is extremely challenging. So the success criteria for any nutritional supplement include providing key nutrients, having very little reliance on other supplies, being ultra simple to administer, and being straightforward to send out to distant locales. Moreover, it has to taste acceptable to the afflicted population.

F-100, the current approach, did little of this. While it did contain nutrients, it had to be constituted with clean water, which is often in short supply in crisis spots. Similarly, charcoal and propane can be limited in these contexts, so any new solution needed to avoid the heating that F-100 required. Another issue was that F-100 had to be consumed almost immediately. That meant there were operational inefficiencies, and the powder couldn't be sent out far from distribution centers. Furthermore, it required clean vessels to consume the mixture and training to prepare it according to precise criteria. The result was that feeding was mainly confined to inpatient nutrition centers where children might stay for about a month, a hardship for families and a drain on strapped agencies as well. Oftentimes, the neediest children never made it to the centers, and far too many people died as a result.

Briend thought about how to solve for these issues, and he created a chocolate bar. While that addressed F-100's issues, it ran into its own obstacle: It melted. So he reframed his perspective and watched what his own children did. One of their favorite foods was the hazelnut spread Nutella, and he saw how they could put it on just about anything to make it more enticing. Inspired, he developed Plumpy'Nut, a substance that tasted like peanut butter and was easy for children to quickly get used to. He also knew that peanuts are a staple of the diet in West Africa, where many crises occur, and so it would be readily taken up there. An obstacle to adoption of past solutions, such as shipping in bulgur wheat from North America, was that they had no basis in the local diet and were rejected, even by a hungry population. Plumpy'Nut paste tastes familiar, requires no preparation or training, is highly portable, and has a two-year shelf life.

Since its creation in 1997, Plumpy'Nut has been used by hundreds of thousands of children in places like Niger, South Sudan, and Malawi, with a success rate estimated from 90 to 95 percent. Because it responds to key jobs to be done and adheres to clear success criteria while circumventing obstacles to adoption it has been a runaway success.

KEEP ASKING WHY

Plumpy'Nut was created by a well-trained and experienced specialist. What about the vast majority of people who lack such skills? How can they innovate?

The U.S. military, while it contains many highly qualified individuals, comprises mainly people who lack much development training. As the military has gotten more involved in nation building abroad, international aid agencies have had to think creatively about how young men and women trained for war can become agents of peace. Armed with budgets in the billions, when the U.S. military decides to become involved in an area of operation, it has a huge impact.

The United States Agency for International Development (USAID) took up the challenge in Afghanistan of figuring out how to make the military more effective nation builders. Working through its Office of Civil-Military Cooperation, it came up with a program that quickly got enlisted men and women working effectively with Afghan communities on development programs, aiming to win the hearts and minds of the people.

The program, called the District Stability Framework, was the brainchild of Dr. James Derleth, a senior stabilization advisor for USAID. Derleth recognized the need to have a simple, replicable process that could be used by both the young private as well as the commanding colonel. At the same time, he was extremely wary of one-size-fits-all efforts in a country as complex as Afghanistan, so military forces would need to tailor their approaches to local communities. To add complication, the military was being asked to play a noncombative role in an often hostile country, and troops were not typically coached in the art of conversation.

Derleth framed the approach succinctly: "Act like a three-year-old and ask 'why, why, why?'" Starting from four simple questions that anyone could base a discussion around, soldiers would probe on the "why" in order to understand the true needs in a district. This approach uncovered jobs in a streamlined fashion. Instead of having long, rambling conversations as many development workers do or fielding surveys that can have no follow-up, the military was uncovering what jobs people wanted to get done. For example, a conversation about the need for water and demands for a well evolved into what people wanted to get done with the water—crop irrigation, human consumption, use for animals—and that opened up a new set of solutions that previously would not be available by focusing on just building that well. The tools enabled even a 20-year-old private to have a meaningful, productive conversation leading directly to activity.

FLEXIBILITY WITHIN STRUCTURE

Aid and development organizations cannot be limitlessly flexible and responsive. While the vast majority of money spent on these purposes goes to good ends, the tiny fraction of projects that go awry generate oceans of bad publicity. As in a large corporation, aid agencies must have rules, structure, and accountability so that disasters are avoided. Creativity cannot be endless.

Within those constraints, Jobs to be Done opens up degrees of freedom. Rather than issuing extensive guidelines about precisely what solutions should be supplied to communities, the Jobs framework enables organizations to ask the right questions in a rigorous and repeatable way. Solutions can then be mapped to very specific findings. If it works for an entity as large as the U.S. military in Afghanistan, the approach can provide major benefits to smaller groups as well.

This sort of discipline also helps organizations become more innovative. While they are frequently told to embrace innovation, nonprofit and public agencies can struggle to do so when their funding is tied tightly to purse masters' programming guidelines. The funders can bolster innovation by giving tightly defined briefs about jobs to address without becoming overly narrow in the solutions they seek. For their part, recipient organizations can use Jobs to be Done to get closer to their end customers (or "stakeholders," as they're often termed), providing a structured and scalable means of gaining input from the field that opens avenues to new solutions by framing the challenges holistically and in great detail. The method helps groups go beyond superficial programming and into meeting deeper needs.

The Jobs Roadmap provides a well-defined process to go from broad mandates to creative yet robust initiatives. That is precisely what nonprofit and governmental groups require so that they avoid missteps while aiding the right people in the right ways.

NOTES

INTRODUCTION

1 Patrick Vlaskovits, "Henry Ford, Innovation, and That 'Faster Horse' Quote," *HBR Blog Network*, August 29, 2011.

2 "Growth Process Toolkit—New Product Development: Accelerating Growth Through Unbiased and Rigorous Early-Stage Product Evaluation," Frost & Sullivan, March 2013.

CHAPTER 1

1 Lucas Matney, "Snapchat Reaches 6 Billion Daily Videos Views, Tripling from 2 Billion in May," *TechCrunch*, November 9, 2015.

2 Steven Johnson, *How We Got to Now: Six Innovations That Made the Modern World*, Riverhead, 2014.

3 Chris Kocek, "Beats $3.2B Sale Proves It's Great, but Not Necessarily at Headphones," *Entrepreneur*, July 18, 2014.

4 Massachusetts Cultural Resource Information System, Massachusetts Historical Commission, as of November 11, 2014.

CHAPTER 2

1 Mike Mancini, "Building Loyalty—One High Profit Customer Segment at a Time," *Nielsen*, August 5, 2009.

2 Tom Post, "America's Best and Worst Franchises," *Forbes*, May 27, 2014.

CHAPTER 3

1 Dina Spector, "The 11 Biggest Food Flops of All Time," *Business Insider*, January 12, 2012.

2 Taddy Hall and Rob Wengel, "Nielsen Breakthrough Innovation Report," The Nielsen Company, June 2014.

CHAPTER 4

1 Taddy Hall and Rob Wengel, "Nielsen Breakthrough Innovation Report," The Nielsen Company, June 2014.

2 "Consumer Reports' Top Picks 2014—The Best Cars, SUVs, and Trucks in 10 Categories," *Consumer Reports*, April 2014. "10 Top Picks of 2015—Best Cars and SUVs from Our Tests," *Consumer Reports*, February 2015.

3 James Vincent, "Tesla's Model S P85D Is So Good It Broke Consumer Reports' Rating System," *The Verge*, August 27, 2015.

4 Eugene Kim, "Slack Just Raised Another $200 Million Round, and It's Now Worth $3.8 Billion," *Business Insider*, April 1, 2016.

5 Jeff Bercovici, "Pew Study Finds MSNBC the Most Opinionated Cable News Channel by Far," *Forbes*, March 18, 2013.

6 Dominic Patten, "Fox News Tops 2012 Cable News Network Ratings; MSNBC Up Big," *Deadline*, December 13, 2012.

CHAPTER 5

1 Max Chafkin, "Is This the Jeff Bezos of Russia?" *Fast Company*, August 8, 2012.

2 Nicola Clark, "Harrods Launches £30 Poulet et Champignon Pot Noodle," *BrandRepublic*, March 13, 2008.

3 Erin Coe, "Risk of 'Patent Troll' Insurance May Slow Adoption," *Law360*, April 22, 2013.

4 Interview with Brendan McSheffrey, en-Gauge CEO, December 2015.

5 "Frustrated Buyers Return Hard-to-Use Gadgets," *Consumer Reports News*, August 26, 2009.

CHAPTER 6

1 Fortune Editors, "Bar Wars: Hershey Bites Mars (Fortune, 1985)," *Fortune*, December 22, 2013.

2 Hershey also tried launching its Simple Pleasures product line in 2012, but it was discontinued in 2014. Hershey (and market analysts) continue to show confidence in the Brookside brand. Elaine Watson, "Hershey 'Very Excited' About Mystery New Product, Reckons Brookside Could be $500M Brand," *Food Navigator*, January 31, 2014. Leading up to its launch of SoFit—a healthy snack brand launched in 2016—Hershey expanded its Brookside offerings with the launch of a new fruit-and-nut bar line.

3 While independent game publishers are free to set their own prices, many of the blockbuster console games will follow the established industry pricing patterns. Lesser known game makers would have a difficult time adopting a strategy that necessitates their selling high-priced games that compete against those of industry incumbents. For more on video game pricing, see Kate Cox, "The Competition Is as Fake as the Blood: Why New Video Games Are Always the Same Price," *Consumerist*, March 15, 2014.

4 Chung Joo-won, "Korea Best Testbed for Senior Care Products," *The Korea Herald*, September 9, 2013.

CHAPTER 7

1 Danielle Sacks, "Oreo Tags Pop Culture," *Fast Company*, November 2014.

2 Peter Drucker, *Managing for Results*, Harper & Row, 1964.

3 Robyn Bolton, "5 New Rules for a Winning Brand Launch," *Fast Company*, March 7, 2012.

CHAPTER 8

1 Brian Dolan, "Fitbit Has Sold Almost 30M Devices Total, Added Nearly 180 Employees in Q3," *MobiHealthNews*, November 5, 2015.

2 Sophie Charara, "Fitbit CEO: Apple Watch 'Probably Does Too Much,'" *Wareable*, April 4, 2016.

3 A. G. Lafley and Roger L. Martin, *Playing to Win*, Harvard Business Review Press, 2013.

4 Paint Nite is a Boston-based start-up founded in 2012. The company offers nightly painting workshops for groups, during which a professional artist provides step-by-step instructions on how to paint a particular piece. Participants drink, socialize, and create their own paintings. The start-up raised $13 million in Series A funding in 2015. Sara Castellanos, "Social Painting Startup Paint Nite Raises $13M in Funding," *Boston Business Journal*, February 23, 2015.

5 This concept draws on the desirable/discussable/unthinkable framework put forth by Stephen's former colleagues at Innosight in their excellent 2008 book, *The Innovator's Guide to Growth: Putting Disruptive Innovation to Work*.

CHAPTER 9

1 Jillian D'Onfro, "There's a Funny Reason People Didn't Understand How to Use Google When It First Launched," *Business Insider*, April 13, 2015.

2 Graeme Wood, "Anthropology Inc.," *Atlantic*, March 2013.

3 Ibid.

4 Clayton M. Christensen, Scott D. Anthony, Gerald Berstell, and Denise Nitterhouse, "Finding the Right Job for Your Product," *MIT Sloan Management Review*, April 1, 2007.

5 Forbes company profiles: http://www.forbes.com/companies/kleenex/

6 Taddy Hall and Rob Wengel, "Nielsen Breakthrough Innovation Report," The Nielsen Company, June 2014.

CHAPTER 10

1 https://www.youtube.com/watch?v=Pmq1MK00000000000000000N1arc

2 Rebecca Greenfield, "Brainstorming Doesn't Work; Try This Technique Instead," *Fast Company*, July 29, 2014.

3 The focus on quantity over structure isn't limited to brainstorming. We've seen many companies launch idea collection platforms and voting portals with the

goal of getting everyone to participate or finding the one-in-a-million idea that will make it all worth it. But ideas frequently lack definition or relevance to the company's plans, judging panels get overwhelmed trying to guess which idea is the best, and the platform quickly becomes an unproductive activity generator. A principle result is cynicism. Much like with brainstorming, these platforms need focus. While they may have a place in innovation, they need to align with the best practices we describe throughout this book so that the output ends up aligning with the organization's goals and satisfying important customers' jobs to be done.

CHAPTER 11

1 Barry Jaruzelski and Richard Holman, "Casting a Wide Net: Building the Capabilities for Open Innovation," *Ivey Business Journal*, March/April 2011.

2 Stephen Wunker, *Capturing New Markets: How Smart Companies Create Opportunities Others Don't*, McGraw-Hill Education, 2011.

3 Abha Bhattarai, "With New Restaurant Incubator, Marriott Hopes to Tap into Local Food Scene," *Washington Post*, January 11, 2015.

4 Interview with Stephen Brickley, November 24, 2015.

CHAPTER 12

1 John McDermott, "Why Ruffles Moved Its Entire Ad Budget to Digital," *Digiday*, November 25, 2014.

2 Alison Millington, "PepsiCo to Move Money into Shopper Marketing and Digital to Maintain Sales Success," *Marketing Week*, February 11, 2015.

3 Dan Ariely, "Why Businesses Don't Experiment," *Harvard Business Review*, April 2010.

4 Janet Adamy, "For McDonald's, It's a Wrap," *Wall Street Journal*, January 30, 2007.

5 Stefan Thomke and Jim Manzi, "The Discipline of Business Experimentation," *Harvard Business Review*, December 2014.

6 Stephanie Strom, "TV Dinners in a Netflix World," *New York Times*, August 31, 2015.

7 Devindra Hardawar, "This Huge Early iPhone Prototype Had a 5-by-7 Inch Screen and a Plethora of Ports," *VentureBeat*, March 11, 2013.

ABOUT THE AUTHORS

STEPHEN WUNKER

Stephen Wunker is the managing director of New Markets Advisors. As a specialist in new markets, Stephen combines world-class strategy consulting and entrepreneurial skills. He is the author of *Capturing New Markets: How Smart Companies Create Opportunities Others Don't*, named one of the five Best Business Books of 2011. Stephen has a long track record of creating successful ventures for his own companies and on behalf of clients.

As a consultant, Stephen was a long-term colleague of Harvard Business School Professor Clayton Christensen in building up his innovation consulting practice, Innosight. He has cowritten two articles with Professor Christensen and helped to put together his book on health care, *The Innovator's Prescription*. He also spent several years consulting at Bain & Company in its Boston and London offices. He founded New Markets Advisors in 2009. In that capacity, he publishes frequently in outlets such as *Forbes*, *Harvard Business Review*, and *The Financial Times*. He has also appeared on Bloomberg and BBC television, and he has been a guest lecturer at Dartmouth's Tuck School of Business.

As an entrepreneur and corporate venturer, Stephen has cofounded Yowzit, the leading Internet site for ratings and reviews in Africa. Previously, he was managing director of Celpay, a mobile commerce start-up created by the pan-African cellular network Celtel, which was sold to the South African financial services group FirstRand. He also served as Celtel's business development director prior to the company being sold to Zain of Kuwait. Additionally, he was CEO of Brainstorm, a developer of mobile software that acquired a start-up he founded, Saverfone. In that capacity he co-founded what is now the global Mobile Marketing Association, and he was a pioneer in the development of the mobile marketing industry. Immediately after he left Bain, Steve joined the British electronics firm Psion PLC and, in a joint venture with Motorola, led the development of one of the world's first smartphones.

Stephen has an MBA from Harvard Business School, a master's of public administration from Columbia University, and a BA cum laude from Princeton University.

JESSICA WATTMAN

Dr. Jessica Wattman is the director of social innovation at New Markets Advisors. Jessica is a veteran at creating strategies for environments in rapid flux. Her work has been predominantly in the public and nonprofit sectors, where she has deployed the Jobs to be Done and other innovation methodologies to create a wide range of trailblazing programs in conflict and other unstable environments.

Her background includes time in Afghanistan, Ethiopia, Lebanon, Zimbabwe, and other hot spots. She has worked for organizations such as the United Nations Development Programme, Save the Children, Oxfam, the United States Agency for International Development, and Mercy Corps. Jessica has extensive experience in conducting primary research and using those findings to create new approaches to facilitate communities' adoption of new ideas. Her media coverage includes a feature story on the CBS Evening News, and she was recently a speaker at the MIT Media Lab. In addition to her public and nonprofit work, Jessica has deployed these innovation methodologies for private sector clients, working with New Markets since 2010 for clients in industries including online education and Internet services.

Jessica is a magna cum laude graduate of Columbia University's Barnard College. She also has a master's in public policy from Harvard University's John F. Kennedy School of Government and a PhD in political science from the Massachusetts Institute of Technology. She is fluent in Spanish and French, and she has lived on four continents.

DAVID FARBER

Dave Farber is a manager at New Markets Advisors, specializing in growth strategy and innovation. His work focuses on helping companies find organic sources of growth and capture value through new business models. This work includes launching new products, attracting new customers, and exploring new markets. Dave has extensive experience using the Jobs to be Done framework to find new growth opportunities, having yielded successful results for clients spanning four continents and a wide range of industries. In addition to conducting Jobs-based research on behalf of his clients, Dave has also helped companies build their own innovation capabilities by leveraging the Jobs framework and other innovation best practices.

Dave is also a licensed Massachusetts attorney. Prior to joining New Markets, his work focused on external sources of growth, including M&A transactions, strategic partnerships, and start-up advisory services. His experience included time at leading law firms in the United States and Belgium. He also spent time at Brookfield Renewable Power, providing legal advice and strategic guidance to senior management.

Dave is a magna cum laude graduate of Villanova Law School, where he was a managing editor of the *Villanova Law Review*. He is also a magna cum laude graduate of American University.

INDEX

CPSIA information can be obtained
at www.ICGtesting.com
Printed in the USA
LVHW091416030223
738601LV00007B/56

9 781400 238767